Worship
CHANGES / EVERYTHING

Worship

DARLENE ZSCHECH

CHANGES EVERYTHING

EXPERIENCING

God's Presence

IN EVERY MOMENT *of* LIFE

BETHANY HOUSE PUBLISHERS

a division of Baker Publishing Group
Minneapolis, Minnesota

Published by Bethany House Publishers
11400 Hampshire Avenue South
Bloomington, Minnesota 55438
www.bethanyhouse.com

Bethany House Publishers is a division of
Baker Publishing Group, Grand Rapids, Michigan

Printed in the United States of America

ISBN 978-0-7642-1427-1 (cloth)
ISBN 978-0-7642-1499-8 (international trade paper)

Library of Congress Cataloging-in-Publication Data
Zschech, Darlene.
    Worship changes everything : experiencing God's presence in every moment of life / Darlene Zschech.
        pages cm
        Summary: "A Christian singer and songwriter presents a definition of worship and shares with readers how to let wonder and worship pervade their daily lives"— Provided by publisher.
    1. Worship. I. Title.
    BV10.3.Z73 2015
    248.3—dc23   2015016129

Cover and interior design by Peter Gloege | LOOK Design Studio

Author is represented by Iconic Media Brands

15 16 17 18 19 20 21   7 6 5 4 3 2 1

To all those who have valiantly gone before . . .
announcing and declaring
the goodness and presence of God.

BOOKS BY
DARLENE ZSCHECH

Extravagant Worship

The Kiss of Heaven

The Art of Mentoring

Revealing Jesus

CONTENTS

ACKNOWLEDGMENTS

To all who have contributed to this manuscript, with all my heart I say thank you.

To my strong tower of a husband, Mark; to my world-changing children and grandchildren; to Mark Gilroy; and to our loving and prayerful church family HopeUC . . . I am as grateful as one can be.

In the end, with all that I am I say . . .

All glory to God, all praise to His holy name.

My prayer is that at the end of this book, you find yourself more in love with Jesus.

Love, your friend,

WHEN GOD COMES CLOSE

Sing to God a brand-new song.
He's made a world of wonders!
He rolled up his sleeves,
He set things right.
God made history with salvation,
He showed the world what he could do.

Shout your praises to God, everybody!
Let loose and sing! Strike up the band!

Let ocean breakers call out, "Encore!"
And mountains harmonize the finale—
A tribute to God when he comes,
When he comes to set the earth right.
He'll straighten out the whole world,
He'll put the world right, and everyone in it.

Psalm 98:1-2, 4, 8-9 THE MESSAGE

WHAT IS WORSHIP? Worship is our response to His majesty . . . and as Eugene Peterson so magnificently put it, "A tribute to God when He comes." Worship is the created—you and I—responding to the Creator. Our spirit being fueled in His presence as we invite the river of life to do in us what only He can do.

God's presence defines us; we need more of Him. If you can casually meander through worship, then I would dare to say that maybe, just maybe, you have not entered into true worship at all. We need Jesus-centered, Holy Spirit-filled, passionately led worship. Because when God comes close, everything changes.

Suddenly, God's angel stood among them and God's glory blazed around them. They were terrified. The angel said, "Don't be afraid. I'm here to announce a great and joyful event that is meant for everybody, worldwide: A Savior has just been born in David's town, a Savior who is Messiah and Master. This is what you're to look for: a baby wrapped in a blanket and lying in a manger." At once the angel was joined by a huge angelic choir singing God's praises: Glory to God in the heavenly heights, peace to all men and women on earth who please him.

Luke 2:9-14 The Message

As the angel announced Jesus' birth, all of heaven joined in worship. Later, when the wise men came and saw the child in the arms of Mary, they were overcome and kneeled and worshiped Jesus. These men were truly wise, for when they encountered the long-awaited Savior, their response was to worship.

When Paul and Silas decided to declare God's faithfulness toward them in a prison cell, their response was to worship. God was close, even in the midst of the trial. If we draw near to Him, He will always draw near to us (see James 4:8).

When the woman at the well met Jesus, she was feeling isolated, downtrodden, rejected, and hungry for something more— her heart longed to worship the promised King. When she encountered Him, her life was changed forever. Her worship found its intent. Her worship found its home (see John 4).

When we worship Jesus, we declare His kingdom and announce *His* presence. When we worship, we come by grace through faith, bringing the voice of our hearts before heaven. When we worship, we dispel the darkness and take authority over principalities and powers. When we worship, we exalt Christ and His dominion over every situation and circumstance. When we worship, thanksgiving is our entry point, joy is our strength, and breakthrough is our inheritance. When we worship, demons tremble and angels join in. When we worship, kingdom dominion is established in our lives.

It was God's passion for us that caused Him to send Jesus to us and for us. From that standpoint alone, we worship.

> It all happened in a moment, a most remarkable moment. As moments go, that one appeared no different from any other. . . . It was one of the countless moments that have marked time since eternity became measurable.
>
> But in reality, that particular moment was like none other. For through that segment of time a spectacular thing occurred. God became a man. While the creatures of earth walked unaware, Divinity arrived. Heaven opened herself and placed her most precious one in a human womb.
>
> The omnipotent, in one instant, made himself breakable. He who had been spirit became pierceable. He who was larger than the universe became an embryo. And he who sustains the world with a word chose to be dependent upon the nourishment of a young girl.
>
> God as a fetus. Holiness sleeping in a womb. The creator of life being created. . . . God had come near.
>
> Max Lucado[1]

With all my heart I pray that as you read these pages, you will be filled with wonder yet again at the beauty and faithfulness of our God, and that you will be reminded to see that *worship changes everything.*

Darlene

THE HEART OF

PART ONE

Worship

But the time is coming—indeed it's here now— when true worshipers will worship the Father in spirit and in truth. The Father is looking for those who will worship him that way. For God is Spirit, so those who worship him must worship in spirit and in truth.

JOHN 4:23-24

Our lives are changed forever when we worship God for all He is worth with all we are worth.

CHAPTER 1

HE IS WORTHY

Honor the Lord, you heavenly beings;
honor the Lord for his glory and strength.
Honor the Lord for the glory of his name.
Worship the Lord in the splendor of his holiness.

PSALM 29:1-2

I HAVE FLOWN A LOT OF MILES in the past twenty years, so not surprisingly, I take many things about the experience for granted. For example, when the flight attendants give safety instructions, I find myself switching off—I've heard them many times before and might be able to get on the intercom and recite them myself from memory.

One particular flight was one of those long international routes that you have to prepare for. Even though I quite enjoy them, many hours in a plane can wear you down. A book to read? Check. A second book to read? Check. A movie to watch? Check. I was ready.

There was a family with a little guy of about four years old sitting behind me. I opened my book so the time would pass more swiftly. But as we thundered down the runway, lifted off, and started climbing, the little boy got very excited and said loudly, "Wow, Daddy! I can see the whole world from up here!"

That brought a smile to my lips. I wasn't the only one who put down what I was doing to take another look out the window. His

15

exhilaration and enthusiasm over what was a new experience for him were contagious. In fact, I stopped what I was doing to take another look.

My family and I now live on the stunning Central Coast of Australia. It is a place of both nuanced and stark beauty. I will look out at the ocean from a rocky outcropping and ooh and aah at the beauty of the waves and shore. I will occasionally get a funny look from someone who has spent their whole life in this area. They'll smile and thank me for reminding them to see the awesome beauty of what has become commonplace to them.

I'm like the little boy on the airplane, getting excited and saying for all to hear, "Take another look!"

Is it possible we have become so comfortably blessed and familiar with the grandeur of God, with the holiness of His presence, with the consistency of His goodness in our lives, that we take Him for granted? Is it time we put down what we are doing to take another look?

When is the last time you looked at God and marveled at His beauty and kindness and power and goodness and said "Wow!"?

It's time to look again and see just how wonderful and worthy He truly is!

GOD'S WORTH-SHIP

The word *worship* comes from the old English word that means "worth-ship." Doesn't that make worship simple and clear? We worship God because He is so worthy. We give God His due. All honor and worth belong to Him.

When I consider this, I can feel overwhelmed by the responsibility to honestly bring all that I am to respond to His greatness. But when I look upon the beauty of Jesus, it is there that *worth*-ship becomes so natural—no effort required in His great presence—as my heart simply responds to all of His goodness. He is, after all, the One.

The one who created a beautiful world for us to live in (see Genesis 1-2) spoke everything into existence with just the sound of His voice. "For when he spoke, the world began! It appeared at his command" (Psalm 33:9). Just look around you at the beauty and wonder of the world God created, from the roaring of the sea to the countless stars lighting an azure sky to the tiniest insect to a field of flowers to a towering mountain. Could that have been by accident? Not in a million or even a billion years!

He is the one who created you with purpose and eternal value—you truly are marvelous in all ways. "Thank you for making me wonderfully complex! Your workmanship is marvelous— how well I know it" (Psalm 139:14). You are no accident. You know you have been created as a unique and special person. Born *on* purpose, for purpose.

He is the one who is not only the all-powerful Creator, but eternally faithful and good to us. . . . "He is good! His faithful love endures forever" (Psalm 136:1).

He is the one who is so generous and lavish in His blessings to us. . . . "What can I give back to God for the blessings He has poured out on me?" (Psalm 116:12 THE MESSAGE).

He is the one who planned and gave all for our salvation— even when we rejected and rebelled against Him.

> When we were utterly helpless, Christ came at just the right time and died for us sinners. Now, most people would not be willing to die for an upright person, though someone might perhaps be willing to die for a person who is especially good. But God showed his great love for us by sending Christ to die for us while we were still sinners.
>
> **Romans 5:6-8**

The perfect, spotless, precious Lamb was slain for our sins (see Revelation 5:9-12). When we didn't have a prayer in the world, God gave us a prayer in His Son, Jesus Christ!

He stands alone as the One, the only true God, the King of Kings. Wherever else we might look for worth, greatness, majesty—it can never deliver what it promises.

> At just the right time Christ will be revealed from heaven by the blessed and only almighty God, the King of all kings and Lord of all lords. He alone can never die, and he lives in light so brilliant that no human can approach him. No human eye has ever seen him, nor ever will. All honor and power to him forever! Amen.
>
> **1 Timothy 6:15-16**

There is so much more to be said of God's worth-ship, of how worthy He is to be praised. His wisdom. His kindness. His presence. His healing.

Yet how easy it is to take His faithfulness for granted. None of us like being taken for granted. We want those in our lives to recognize and appreciate us, to respond to the value we bring to them. Our relationships suffer when we are discounted or when we discount others. But it happens. We get self-absorbed, preoccupied, distracted.

Here is your call to not take God for granted. To call you from the distractions and self-absorption that would rob us of experiencing His majesty and greatness in every moment. Take another look.

WORSHIP RESPONDS TO GREATNESS

Tom Wells said it so well:

> Worship is a response to greatness. A man does not become a worshipper merely by saying, "Now I shall become a worshipper." That is impossible. That cannot be done. A man becomes a worshipper when he sees something great that calls forth his admiration or his worship. That is the only way worshippers are made. Worship answers to greatness.[1]

Worship is a response to the revelation of just how great God is. Do you recognize how worthy, how loving, how magnificent He is? His glory and strength, the splendor of His holiness? His saving and incomparable grace?

His glory is rising as the waters cover the seas; worship is being released across the earth like never before, from the temporal to the eternal, from age to age and generation to generation . . . the human heart giving voice to the deepest longing of our souls. Saints and angels join in this heavenly realm.

> Then I looked again, and I heard the voices of thousands and millions of angels around the throne and of the living beings and the elders. And they sang in a mighty chorus: "Worthy is the Lamb who was slaughtered—to receive power and riches and wisdom and strength and honor and glory and blessing."
>
> Revelation 5:11-12

This heart song is not just reserved for heaven. A day is coming when *all the world* will see Jesus for who He is—for all He is worth—for all His glory. Yes, the entire world, no exceptions, will worship because they will finally and ultimately recognize His worthiness:

> And then I heard every creature in heaven and on earth and under the earth and in the sea. They sang: "Blessing and honor and glory and power belong to the one sitting on the throne and to the Lamb forever and ever."
>
> Revelation 5:13

DISCOVERING WHO WE WERE CREATED TO BE

So why do we worship? Because He is worthy. Period. His worthship is all the reason we need.

In our popular culture, we are trained to want to know what we are going to get out of any deal before we agree to it.

Amazingly, some people try to apply that to worship. They want to know if worship is worth it.

If I worship, what do I get? What's in it for me? I want to make sure I like the payback before I start.

Because God is worthy—worth it—we learn that "what's in it for me?" is not a question worth asking. But this is where it gets interesting. Even if the question is self-serving, and even if we know better than to ask, God has provided an answer that is simple and obvious and profound. That's how gracious He is. He answers a question we should never ask, and tells us that when we worship we get the only thing that matters in eternity, and the one thing that fulfills our purpose: *When we worship, we get to experience why we were created—we get to experience Him!*

Experiencing God is why we were created. It is embedded in our DNA. It is the only path to true peace and purpose and fulfillment. Worship lets us experience the Great One—and in the experience discover who we were meant to be.

In *The Purpose Driven Life*, a book that changed so many lives, Pastor Rick Warren wrote:

> You cannot arrive at your life's purpose by starting with a focus on yourself. You must begin with God, your Creator. You exist only because God wills that you exist. You were made by God and for God—and until you understand that, life will never make sense. It is only in God that we discover our origin, our identity, our meaning, our purpose, our significance, and our destiny. Every other path leads to a dead end.[2]

I can't tell you all the ways your life will change. I can't tell you the new adventures that will open before you. I can simply promise you that you will find your Creator is worthy. Your worship is important because He is worthy!

David is a man from Scripture who has inspired many of us in our approach to our faith and worship. His life was not easy and his conduct was not perfect, but he was a man who knew God's heart and made it his own (see Acts 13:22).

All of us know about his battle with Goliath, but Goliath wasn't the only giant David faced. In 2 Samuel 21:16, we read that he was trapped by Ishbi-benob: "Ishbi-benob was a descendant of the giants; his bronze spearhead weighed more than seven pounds, and he was armed with a new sword. He had cornered David and was about to kill him." David was saved by his boyhood friend Abishai, but the man after God's heart knew deep down it was God himself who saved him.

The story of Ishbi-benob is a snapshot in the video of David's life. At each crucial moment, David turned to God—for help, for forgiveness, for salvation, for renewal. His petitions for mercy and rescue were so heartfelt that they become visceral for us. We actually feel and experience David's emotions—his pain, fears, joys, and hopes—in the reading of his words.

But whatever snapshot we look at from David's life—fighting giants, dancing before the Lord, leading armies, showing mercy to his enemy—we discover that the deepest, most pervasive, most inspiring thoughts and emotions of his life were his experiences of God's majesty. It is all about Him. When we say yes to life *in* Christ, our lives are lived *in* Him. Every victory is His. Every task and every word is for His glory. David knew what was due to God, and it was everything. He knew it wasn't about him, about what he went through or accomplished. It was about God. David's life and worship was built on the worthiness of God. The refrain echoes through his writings.

David sang this song to the Lord on the day the Lord rescued him from all his enemies and from Saul. He sang: "The Lord is my rock, my fortress, and my savior; my God is my rock, in whom I find protection. He is my shield, the power that saves me, and my place of safety. He is my refuge, my savior, the one who saves me from violence. I called on the Lord, who is worthy of praise, and he saved me from my enemies."

2 Samuel 22:1-4

I called on the Lord, who is worthy of praise, and he saved me
from my enemies.

Psalm 18:3

Great is the Lord! He is most worthy of praise! He is to be
feared above all gods.

Psalm 96:4

Great is the Lord! He is most worthy of praise! No one can
measure his greatness.

Psalm 145:3

YOU ARE INVITED

God is worthy, but what about us? What makes us worthy to worship? Isaiah reminds us we can't worship based on our own worthiness: "A voice said, 'Shout!' I asked, 'What should I shout?' 'Shout
that people are like the grass. Their beauty fades as quickly as the
flowers in a field'" (Isaiah 40:6).

John the Baptist realized he was not worthy of Jesus: "Though
his ministry follows mine, I'm not even worthy to be his slave and
untie the straps of his sandal" (John 1:27). If someone as powerful
and righteous as John is not worthy of Jesus, what hope is there
for us?

Paul echoed John the Baptist when he said, "For I am the
least of all the apostles. In fact, I'm not even worthy to be called
an apostle after the way I persecuted God's church" (1 Corinthians
15:9). Our lives have not been worthy either. There are things in
our past we are not proud of.

But don't lose heart. We've all been invited to worship.
Through the glorious grace of Jesus Christ, God sees us as perfect.
Jesus tells the story of a wedding banquet:

> "God's kingdom," he said, "is like a king who threw a wedding
> banquet for his son. He sent out servants to call in all the
> invited guests. And they wouldn't come! He sent out another

round of servants, instructing them to tell the guests, 'Look, everything is on the table, the prime rib is ready for carving. Come to the feast!' They only shrugged their shoulders and went off, one to weed his garden, another to work in his shop. The rest, with nothing better to do, beat up on the messengers and then killed them. The king was outraged and sent his soldiers to destroy those thugs and level their city.

"Then he told his servants, 'We have a wedding banquet all prepared but no guests. The ones I invited weren't up to it. Go out into the busiest intersections in town and invite anyone you find to the banquet.' The servants went out on the streets and rounded up everyone they laid eyes on, good and bad, regardless. And so the banquet was on—every place filled."

Matthew 22:1-10 THE MESSAGE

The first group was too self-absorbed and distracted to recognize the feast to which they were invited—a feast to last eternity! But no one in the second group felt worthy of an invite to the heavenly feast either. The only difference was, the second group recognized the worthiness of the King and said, "Yes, I will come."

Jesus ended that story with the haunting words, "That's what I mean when I say, 'Many get invited; only a few make it'" (v. 14).

It's that simple. You and I have been invited to experience God now and for all eternity. The only response required is for us to say yes.

Ephesians 2:20-21 says that "together, we are His house, built on the foundation of the apostles and prophets. And the cornerstone is Christ Jesus himself. We are carefully joined in Him, becoming a holy temple for the Lord."

It's all about Jesus. Always has been, always will be.

SOLI DEO GLORIA

My heart responded in worship when I was just fifteen years old. I was a mess. I felt bad about myself. I blamed myself for so many things, some of them not even within my control. I was unhappy and confused. I had made mistakes, but more importantly, my heart wasn't in a good place. I had no peace. I was on the wrong path in life. But that was the year that everything changed for me. In the midst of worship, in a crystal-clear moment, I heard God speak to my heart and tell me how much He really loved me. I had sensed His presence numerous other times, even as a young child, but this was the defining moment when I fell in love with Jesus and I felt His love for me. Light and love flooded my life, a healing balm flowing straight from heaven. I knew deep in my soul how worthy God was and that I must give Him my everything, starting with my heart.

That was the moment I was invited to a feast and said, "Yes, Lord, yes. Yes. Yes. Yes."

Since that experience, I have never wanted to stop responding to Jesus with love, praise, thanksgiving, and faithfulness. That's why when I think about my life and who I am as a person, my self-definition and understanding always begin with the simple thought, *I worship the one who knows me best and loves me most.* I worship the one who created and redeemed me. Worship is my song, my prayer, my message, my joy, my focus, my everything, my service, because that is where I experienced—and experience daily—the kindness and greatness of God. Worship changed everything for me. It still does.

At my core I am a worshiper of God, and the desire of my heart is to lead others into that transforming experience. In fact, I challenge all of you who are involved in worship ministry and leading others to take some time every day to thank God for all He is and what He has done. Thank Him for the authority and anointing He has placed within you to exalt His name. Thank Him for His miraculous outworking in your daily life, both private and public. These are great days of His power and might. Don't miss them as you lead worship and lead people to the incomparable greatness of God.

The past year has been a hard one for me and my family.

I was diagnosed with and treated for cancer. But I can tell you, our God is so faithful and loving, and the Bible describes Him as our Healer. I also want to share this discovery with you: The presence of God is for all our days and all our situations; the easy-going moments, the victorious moments, and yes . . . the difficult moments. *Especially* the difficult moments. Even on my darkest days, Jesus held me. I pictured God himself singing songs of love over me. Meanwhile, prayer-warrior worship leaders sang and rejoiced over me, and my family and I made a decision to trust God's plan and love for us all in the midst of the suffering.

Acknowledge Him. Recognize His worth. Say yes to the invitation to the feast.

Throughout this book, I will pursue the theme of God's presence—for there is no other starting point. That means *Worship Changes Everything* isn't just about going to church or what happens for a particular hour or two in the week, even though coming together as a body to worship is critical to our spiritual health. This book is about every moment of life and every step of our journey—at work, at home, alone or with others—because God is ever-present and He is truly worthy!

As you read this book, I pray your heart will be stirred by the glory of God and that with every fiber of your being you will recognize and acknowledge Him. It's not enough to know He is great; we must give expression to that thought. Start there.

I close this chapter where I started, with a definition of worship, this one expressed by Bill Thrasher:

> The simplest way to define worship is that it is to attribute worth to God's revealed character. The command to "ascribe to the Lord the glory due to His name" in Psalm 29:2 does not mean we add anything to God. It simply means that we acknowledge Him for who He is and in this way glorify or honor Him. This is precisely what is being done in heaven. . . . [See Revelation 4:11; 5:12.][3]

Soli Deo Gloria. That is the signature Johann Sebastian Bach and others have used on their works of art to let the world know that what they created was for *God's glory alone.*

I pray that same signature is used across the very fabric of our lives.

WORTHY IS THE LAMB

Thank You for the cross Lord
Thank You for the price You paid
Bearing all my sin and shame
In love You came
And gave amazing grace

Thank You for this love Lord
Thank You for the nail pierced hands
Washed me in Your cleansing flow
Now all I know
Your forgiveness and embrace

Worthy is the Lamb
Seated on the throne
We Crown You now with many crowns
You reign victorious
High and lifted up
Jesus Son of God
The Darling of Heaven crucified
Worthy is the Lamb
Worthy is the Lamb[4]

CHAPTER 2

HE IS PRESENT

And without faith it is impossible to please God,
because anyone who comes to him must
believe that he exists and that he rewards
those who earnestly seek him.

HEBREWS 11:6 NIV

HAVE YOU EVER WISHED you could spend time with a particular someone who is hard to reach—perhaps someone who is influential, famous, and powerful—but you know there is very little chance of that ever happening because there are so many walls and barriers erected around the person? There is a lot of celebrity worship in our world today. The fact that many celebrities work so hard to keep their lives private almost seems to add to their allure. They can play a coy game of acting "hard to get."

Our God is so different. He does not lock the gates to keep us out or play emotional games to keep us at a distance. Instead, He throws the gates to himself wide open and invites us in. He doesn't have a secretary answer the phone and tell us He will get back to us when He has a free moment; He hears our every cry—even when we whisper in the night. Our God doesn't ask us to sign up and pay to be in a fan club; he invites us to come freely to His throne room. But He doesn't stop there. He rises from His throne and passes through His gates of majesty and seeks us out, no matter where we're hiding.

It's not just that we have access to God because we want it and need it. We have access to God, we can experience Him, *because He reaches out to us*. He is the Inviter. He is the Divine Visitor into our lives. And what an invitation He has sent. He is saying to us, "Be new, joyful, purpose-driven, victorious, and complete. . . . Be the person I created you to be . . . by experiencing my presence. I am the one who knows you best and loves you most. Open your eyes. Open your heart. Open your spirit. Let your faith take hold of my presence, right here and right now."

BE PRESENT

How many times have we missed something beautiful right in front of us because we were preoccupied? Or just as likely, because we don't *expect* that beautiful thing to be there? In our minds we know God is everywhere. We've been taught that from the time we first heard God's name. Psalm 139 states His nearness wherever we are. We know He isn't confined to a church building or only available at certain times of day. But we can still miss God at work even when He is right in front of our eyes.

Why? Because we have not yet learned the art of knowing and following the voice of the Holy Spirit as He speaks. Two people hear the same song. One experiences God, and one daydreams about something that needs to be done at work next week. Two people face a crisis in life. One experiences an overwhelming sense of grace flood over her in her pain—after all, He is not just present but *very* present help in our time of trouble (see Psalm 46:1)—while the other feels nothing but hurt, betrayal, and loneliness. Why? It's all about how and where we place our faith and expectation. By God's grace, because I have a growing revelation of the love of God toward me, even on the worst of days I am expecting Him to turn it around.

If I can encourage you in one way, it would be for you to cultivate an attitude of expectation so that you will be present in His presence. Don't wait until you have things figured out. Don't wait until you feel spiritual. Expect Him right now. King David said with much confidence in Psalm 27:14, "Wait for the Lord; be strong and take heart and wait for the Lord" (NIV).

Each of us has had conversations with someone when we knew the other person wasn't really *there*. Physically they were there. Words came out of their mouth. They looked in our direction, but we could just tell they weren't present. It is so easy to get distracted and not fully be in the moment. Experience God in the present. He is with us now. Emmanuel, God with us. All you have to do is be aware, whether you are driving in your car, shopping for groceries, reading a bedtime story to your child, waking up and putting the coffee on, or standing with other believers with arms stretched high, singing songs of praise and thanksgiving to your Lord and Savior. He is with us.

One enduring Christian devotional book is *The Practice of the Presence of God* by Brother Lawrence, a seventeenth-century Carmelite monk. It was this precious saint's goal to do nothing out of selfishness, but to do everything out of love for God, whether working the soil or studying God's Word. For him that meant realizing he was always in God's presence and living every moment in that realization. His simple but profound teaching was "to form a habit of conversing with God continually, and referring all we do to Him." What if you do that and still don't feel His presence? Brother Lawrence continues: "We must at first apply to Him with some diligence: but that after a little care we should find His love inwardly excites us to it without any difficulty."[1]

It was early in my Christian experience that my attention and awareness of the presence of God became very real, that I was so aware that if I drew near to Him, He always would draw near to me. He hemmed me in, behind and before. Laid His hand upon me, gently, not heavy-handed. And my heart continues to be overwhelmed by the fact that the God who created the heavens and the earth actually is here *and* delights to draw near.

His presence defines us, sets us apart, strengthens us, penetrates our very being, and brings joy and strength as we draw near.

James 4:8 says, "Draw near to God and He will draw near to you" (NKJV).

The worship of our God—whether we are together in community, in a more private setting, or in our day-to-day walk with God—is a purposeful part of this miracle of being aware, surrounded by, and made strong in His presence.

Psalm 140:13 says, "Surely the righteous shall give thanks to Your name, the upright shall dwell in Your presence [before Your very face]" (NKJV).

1 Chronicles 16:28 says, "Shout Bravo! to God. Families of the peoples, in awe of the Glory, in awe of the strength: Bravo! Shout Bravo! to His famous Name, lift high an offering and enter His presence! Stand resplendent in His robes of holiness!" (THE MESSAGE).

Psalm 100:2 says, "Serve the Lord with gladness; come before His presence with singing" (NKJV).

When we worship and praise, we declare His kingdom and announce His presence!

We come by faith, through Jesus Christ, to adore and exalt and honor and celebrate our King—to magnify Him; to arrest the spirit of the world and with authority proclaim His goodness, dispelling darkness as the song of our hearts announces that greater is He who is in me than he that is in the world! We play, we sing, we dance, we clap, we bow, we shout, we weep, we kneel, we listen, we serve, we love, and we live in Him—all of it to behold Him in His beauty, as we see the power and presence of almighty God revealed in our midst.

Psalm 92:1 says, "What a beautiful thing, God, to give thanks, to sing an anthem to you, the High God! To announce your love each daybreak, and sing your faithful presence all through the night, accompanied by dulcimer and harp, the full-bodied music of strings" (THE MESSAGE).

All I need to do is simply to put myself in a place mentally, emotionally, and spiritually, where I can receive God's incomparable gift of love and mercy through Jesus Christ, in the now, in the present.

A MEETING AT THE WELL

I love the story of the woman at the well and her encounter with Jesus, a passage you are probably already quite familiar with. But if not, it is one I would suggest you read now (found in John 4). As happens when I pour my heart into the Word of God, the more I meditate on a passage—even a familiar passage—the more I see and learn. The heart of this story reveals the longing of our hearts to experience God and His majesty, but also the reality that far too often we resist His presence.

It's fascinating that Jesus' followers never noticed this woman. They walked right by as if they didn't see her. In their self-importance and self-concern—and certainly due to their conditioned response to look down on Samaritans and especially women—maybe they really didn't take her in. But Jesus did. And He didn't wait for her to acknowledge Him. He spoke first. He took the initiative. That's the love of our heavenly Father in action, meeting us just where we are in our lives.

Jesus wasn't reaching out to someone the world considers important and special. To the contrary, if anyone had reason to feel badly about the circumstances of their lives, it was this Samaritan woman—a member of a despised community. But she was at the bottom of the pecking order even there. She was drawing water at the hottest part of the day when she was sure to be alone, protected from the judgmental glances and cutting remarks of the other women. They had undoubtedly come to the well during the coolest part of the day. It was a time of work and socializing. This woman was not invited. She was an outcast among outcasts.

Not only was she an outcast, but she had lost at love. The Samaritan woman had been married five times and was now living with a sixth man. Whether she lost her previous husbands through death or divorce is beside the point. Either way, can't you imagine her sense of loss, pain, and betrayal when she thought about her relationships that were supposed to be built on love and trust? No wonder she wasn't married. She had failed at love too many times before and wasn't about to trust her heart again; so, unmarried, she moved in with the latest man in her life.

Even if we've never experienced something so dramatic, our lives aren't that different from this woman's. We too have failed. We've felt unloved. We've not been invited to the party. It's humbling to remember that whenever Jesus comes close, whenever God draws near, He sees past all of our mistakes, our failings, our regrets, our sins, our victories and defeats, our highs and lows, and He goes straight to the deeper issues of the heart. Jesus begins a conversation with this woman by asking for a drink of cool, refreshing water, but when the woman shows even a flicker of spiritual response—a seed of faith—He moves to the heart of the matter, asking why she hasn't asked Him for living water.

He's not willing to deal with superficial surface issues with her—or us.

Sometimes our keenest defenses in life are raised to try to keep God away. We fear what His presence would mean in our lives. Some of us hurt so much we struggle mightily to come to the place where we know we are loved and can trust someone else—even God. I believe that was the case with this woman. So she starts a little "worship war" with Jesus. She tries to put Jesus off and keep Him at arm's length by explaining how Samaritans worship—and reminding Him that Jews do things differently. Besides, as a man, He is not even supposed to be speaking to her. There, that should put Jesus in His place.

I can almost see Jesus smiling—but trying not to show it lest she feel disrespected—as He cuts through her verbal defenses by telling her, "The time is coming, yes, it is here now, when the true worshipers will worship the Father in Spirit and in truth" (v. 23 NLV). He speaks of the future—she already acknowledged the

Messiah was coming—but stresses the present, to let her know that the one she is waiting for is here right now, right where she is. And even if she puts up all her defenses, she can't get rid of Him that easily!

It wasn't just the woman who pushed God off into the undefined future. Jesus' disciples did too. When we aren't quite ready to stand in the presence of God, we do the same thing. We put Him off by saying we'll see Him later. But Jesus doesn't want to be put on our waiting list. Later isn't acceptable to Him. That's why He said to His followers—then and now—after this encounter with the woman: "Do you not say, 'It is four months yet until the time to gather grain'? Listen! I say to you, open your eyes and look at the fields. They are white now and waiting for the grain to be gathered in'" (v. 35 NLV).

Patience is a virtue, but we aren't called to wait for something that is already here. I am so much more aware of time and its value the older I get. We cannot get back the time we waste, and each one of us has been placed, on purpose, for such a time as this. God is here now.

I love how in the presence of Jesus this Samaritan woman found exactly who her heart had been longing for. As is the case for us all, to fully accept who you are, you've got to go back to the one who made you—remember that you were created to worship the one who is worthy. And once you understand how valuable you are to Him, once you open your heart to His love with acceptance and faith, your life will never be the same.

My lovely friend, you can sit by the well of regret and self-pity or draw near to the wellspring of life, our Jesus Christ, to whom all worship and praise is due both now and evermore.

WITNESSES OF HIS PRESENCE

It was in the house of God that I encountered Him in such a dramatic, powerful, and personal way. My heart was set free. Not every problem of my life was solved immediately. Troubles and problems will always be part of our earthly existence. But oh how my life was changed. Everything changed.

I physically felt the weight of God's love for me. My mourning met dancing, my sorrow met joy, my insecurity met freedom, my ashes met beauty, my unforgiveness toward others met a redemptive spirit, old things became new, anger and confusion and aimlessness were replaced by a walk of joy and worship in God's presence.

Along with the woman at the well who received living water and ran to share it with others, we too become witnesses to God's goodness. We are experiencing His kingdom come on earth, as it is in heaven, and so we go and share this good news with all who will listen.

Moses lost his family shortly after his birth when the pharaoh of Egypt ordered Hebrew boys to be killed in a despicable act of mass murder. Moses was delivered from the river. He was educated and sophisticated in the way of the Egyptians, but his heart was not at peace. He became a murderer. He became a fugitive. He quit on himself and God. He ran from his God-given destiny to be the leader of God's people, and instead herded sheep in a remote, isolated land. Nothing wrong with herding sheep—that task served David quite well—but it wasn't Moses' calling and destiny. Moses gave up on himself, but God never did. He paid him a special visit, allowing Moses to experience His presence in a fiery bush (see Exodus 3:1-5), which enabled him to do and be what God had planned for him.

Moses was a fighter—he resisted God's presence. But our wonderful God didn't take no for an answer. Even after experiencing the great I Am, Moses let God know that he wasn't the man for the job. "Moses raised another objection to God: 'Master, please, I don't talk well. I've never been good with words, neither before nor after you spoke to me. I stutter and stammer'" (Exodus 4:10 THE MESSAGE). But thankfully He stayed in the moment. He stayed in the presence and heard God speak to him:

"And who do you think made the human mouth? And who makes some mute, some deaf, some sighted, some blind? Isn't it I, God? So, get going. I'll be right there with you—with your mouth! I'll be right there to teach you what to say."

Exodus 4:11-12 The Message

That's so encouraging to me. Even when we are confused and struggle, if we will only stay in the conversation with God, He will take us where we need to go.

Centuries later, God had similar plans for another murderer, another fighter—this one named Saul. He was a hater and persecutor who did his terrible work with zeal and passion (see Philippians 3:6). But then Saul encountered Jesus on the road to Damascus (see Acts 9:1-9). Isn't it fascinating that Saul experienced God's presence, the heart of worship, in the very place he was attacking it? Saul wasn't going to church. Saul was going to murder. But God is so good and so gracious. He knocked Saul off the donkey he was riding; He took his sight from him for a short season; He sent a fearful but faithful servant to minister to him; He did exactly what was needed to turn Saul's life upside down through a divine encounter.

He will do the same for you and me. But before we go too far from the passage in Acts, I want us to back up to chapter 7. There is one other witness I want you to meet. His name is Stephen. He is remembered as the first Christian martyr. Oh, what a spirit he had! He is first mentioned in Acts because of his outstanding service to others. He was chosen by the church to serve as a deacon—taking care of everyday business and the feeding of the widows—so the apostles would be free to preach (see Acts 6:3-6). But the church soon discovered that this servant could preach up a storm as well as anybody. In Acts 7 we read one of the most beautiful and powerful sermons ever given. I would encourage you to read his marvelous words right now.

His words were filled with such power and conviction that those who were at war with God could not stand the sound of them. They covered their ears. They shouted to drown him out. That is resistance!

When his sermon was done, Stephen was taken outside and stoned to death. Saul didn't directly participate in throwing rocks at him, but he obviously approved because he guarded the coats of the murderers. But please don't miss the last words out of Stephen's mouth as the cruel stones crashed against his head and body: "Lord, do not hold this sin against them" (Acts 7:60 NIV). Oh my. How could that be his prayer? He was echoing the words and heart of Jesus on the cross. As Stephen was hit by stones, as he was spit on, as he was taunted and ridiculed, how could he respond with such grace and forgiveness? How could he love in the face of such hatred? If you look at Acts 7:56, he declared, "I see Christ."

Stephen saw Jesus. He was in the presence of God. He experienced the heart of worship, and it changed everything. I believe that through Saul's being in the presence of God, which Stephen displayed for all his tormentors to see, God began the process of change in Saul's wicked heart.

CHRIST WITH ME

Patrick is known as one of Christendom's great missionaries and is the patron saint of Ireland. He was not Irish himself, but a Breton, which basically made him Roman. As a young man Patrick was taken into slavery by the Irish, but he escaped and returned to England, lucky to be alive. But after he was converted to Christ, his heart was immediately drawn to the Irish, the people who had enslaved him. He returned to share Jesus with the people who once abused him and held him captive. Legend tells us that the fierce Irish respected him greatly for a simple reason: He was not afraid of them. His attitude was *I only fear God*. As amazing an attitude as that is, it is still natural to wonder how he could have such a powerful ministry of evangelizing an entire nation of people who had once been his enemies. Perhaps his secret is found in the beautiful words he penned, "Christ Be With Me," also known as his "breastplate"—his protection.

Christ Be With Me

Christ with me, Christ before me, Christ behind me,
Christ in me, Christ beneath me, Christ above me,
Christ on my right, Christ on my left,
Christ where I lie, Christ where I sit, Christ where I arise,
Christ in the heart of every one who thinks of me,
Christ in the mouth of every one who speaks to me,
Christ in every eye that sees me,
Christ in every ear that hears me.
Salvation is of the Lord.
Salvation is of the Christ.
May your salvation, Lord, be ever with us.

There truly is nowhere we can go, no situation, no challenge, no relationship, no conversation where God isn't present. Because of His great love for us, and His spirit at work in and through us, His worship will invade every nook and cranny of our lives.

Psalm 139 was written by David, who truly understood the heart of worship. Read what he says about experiencing God's presence.

God, investigate my life;
    get all the facts firsthand.
I'm an open book to you;
    even from a distance, you know what I'm thinking.
You know when I leave and when I get back;
    I'm never out of your sight.
You know everything I'm going to say
    before I start the first sentence.
I look behind me and you're there,
    then up ahead and you're there, too—
    your reassuring presence, coming and going.

This is too much, too wonderful—
>   I can't take it all in!

Is there any place I can go to avoid your Spirit?
>   To be out of your sight?
If I climb to the sky, you're there!
>   If I go underground, you're there!
If I flew on morning's wings
>   to the far western horizon,
You'd find me in a minute—
>   you're already there waiting!
Then I said to myself, "Oh, he even sees me in the dark!
>   At night I'm immersed in the light!"

Psalm 139:1-11 The Message

There is so much wisdom in the straightforward words of A. W. Tozer:

> The church is famishing for want of his presence. The instant cure of most of our religious ills would be to enter the presence in spiritual experience, to become suddenly aware that we are in God and that God is in us. This would lift us out of our pitiful narrowness and cause our hearts to be enlarged.[2]

Let's go back to the beginning of this chapter. The heart of worship is based on the presence of God. Do you see God in your sitting and standing, in your coming and going, before you and behind you, in your words and in your silence? Acts 17:28 says that "in Him we live and move and have our being" (NKJV). The result of worship is experiencing God. He is always there. It is for us to open our hearts and minds to expect His presence. My prayer for you and me is to see the living God at work in every area of our lives today and always.

CHAPTER 3

HE IS LOVING

*Therefore, I urge you, brothers and sisters, in view of God's mercy,
to offer your bodies as a living sacrifice, holy and pleasing to God—
this is your true and proper worship. Do not conform to the pattern
of this world, but be transformed by the renewing of your mind.
Then you will be able to test and approve what God's will is—
his good, pleasing and perfect will.*

ROMANS 12:1-2 NIV

JESUS LOVES US SO MUCH. And we respond with love to Him.
Like the beautiful worship song written in the early 1900s by an
unknown author reminds us:

> I love Him, I love Him,
> Because He first loved me,
> And purchased my salvation
> On Calv'ry's tree.[1]

"We love Him, because He first loved us" (1 John 4:19 Amplified).
When we open our eyes and really see our Savior, the first thing
we see is just how much He loves us. There is no other starting
place. In one of his trademark impassioned pleas to the church,
Paul spills his heart and makes his confession. He once thought
he could experience God because of his own efforts. He learned
otherwise.

40

> The *real* believers are the ones the Spirit of God leads to work
> away at this ministry, filling the air with Christ's praise as we

do it. We couldn't carry this off by our own efforts, and we know it—even though we can list what many might think are impressive credentials. You know my pedigree: a legitimate birth, circumcised on the eighth day; an Israelite from the elite tribe of Benjamin; a strict and devout adherent to God's law; a fiery defender of the purity of my religion, even to the point of persecuting the church; a meticulous observer of everything set down in God's law Book.

The very credentials these people are waving around as something special, I'm tearing up and throwing out with the trash—along with everything else I used to take credit for. And why? Because of Christ.

Philippians 3:3-7 THE MESSAGE

When we truly worship because God is worthy, because God is present, because of God's great and amazing love, we will all testify with Paul: "We couldn't carry this off by our own efforts, and we know it. . . . I'm throwing in the trash anything and everything I ever took credit for."

The greatest hymn writer of all time, David—the man who knew the heart of God, who was a man after God's own heart (see Acts 13:22)—fully and completely understood his worship was not based on his own efforts, but was based on amazing grace.

> Generous in love—God, give grace!
> Huge in mercy—wipe out my bad record.
> Scrub away my guilt,
> soak out my sins in your laundry.
> I know how bad I've been;
> my sins are staring me down.

Psalm 51:1-3 THE MESSAGE

Worship changes everything because it is being in the presence of the one who is worthy of all worship, and acknowledging that all I am, all that I have, all that I do is a response to His amazing grace.

DO YOU KNOW HOW MUCH
I LOVE YOU?

When the doctor told Mark and me that I had breast cancer, we heard those words with such a mix of emotions. There was fear, certainly. I love my husband, my daughters, and yes, my grandbabies, so much. I was praying before I knew I was praying. *Please, Lord, don't take away my dear ones from me or me from them.* I know that heaven is such a sweet and beautiful place—why be afraid?— but fear tried to stare me down and bring doubt about my future. Somewhere within me during this time, I just knew in my spirit that my time and work here on earth is not done. In the days that followed, as we talked to each other and the children, I experienced so much love from them and other cherished friends that I knew, just knew, that Jesus had won it all, and that He would never leave me or forsake me.

My husband is so strong, and his confidence that God was with us and would bless me beyond measure was faith-building. Perfect love casts out all fear. And this I know to be true. The confidence I have in these words continues to grow within me. And I praise God for a husband who showed great determination that we would work, rest, pray, fight, and do anything and everything God called us to do to experience His healing. I have been so blessed to have family and friends to walk this journey with me. My oldest daughter, Amy, has been a wonderful friend and comfort to me as she has taken care of me. Her tenderness and fierce love toward me still brings tears to my eyes. She still fusses over me to make sure I am okay in every way. Thank you, Amy. I am so, so grateful to God for my family. Zoe kept me laughing, and Chloe kept my feet on the ground.

As I entered into the medical treatments, there were moments of discouragement, frustration, and despair. I hurt. I could hardly think straight. During chemo, I think my emotions shut down for a while. I just felt numb. But as I learned to open my heart again to God's presence and just simply *be* with Him, worship began to flow . . . slowly, but wholeheartedly, and His presence with me is something I treasure more than words can express. God spoke to me in that numbness, not with audible words, but so clearly in my spirit. He asked me, "Darlene, do you trust me?" I weighed my heart and my answer carefully. My answer was soft. I was tired. I didn't feel energy coursing through my body. But my answer was, "Yes, God, I trust you."

That God should come so close to talk with me was enough for me to keep going. But it wasn't enough for God. He wasn't done talking to me. His next question, which went straight to my heart and soul, still overwhelms me. He asked, "Darlene, do you know how much I really love you?"

Tears coursed down my cheeks. I sobbed. I'm a church girl. Of course I know God loves me! I know the Bible verses and the right answers. I knew He loved me so much He gave His only Son—my wonderful Savior—to die for me. But God didn't want me to answer with what I grew up with and what I already knew in my head. He wanted me to know how much He loved me, right then, right there, deep in my heart. To be honest, I was struggling with this question. It didn't feel like love. But in one of the most intimate moments of my life, I gave God my answer. "Yes, I know how much you love me." I did. I do. And because I trust His love for me, I can trust Him with the process.

His presence, His love, overwhelmed me. It hurt him that I was walking through suffering. I am still awed at the moment. I heard Psalm 23 loud and clear within in me—though you walk *through* the shadow of the valley of death. I would walk through. This was a shadow. He would be with me.

Was I still tired? Did I still feel pain? Yes and yes. But oh, in that precious moment of worship, God's love washed over me and inside me. I believe that in that experience I could truly say with Job, "Though He slay me, yet will I trust Him" (Job 13:15 NKJV). I understood David's heart cry when he said,

"O God my rock," I cry,
  "Why have you forgotten me?
Why must I wander around in grief,
  oppressed by my enemies?"
Their taunts break my bones.
  They scoff, "Where is this God of yours?"
Why am I discouraged?
  Why is my heart so sad?
I will put my hope in God!
  I will praise him again—
  my Savior and my God!

Psalm 42:9-11

I am not forgotten. I am loved. I can trust Him with all my heart—and with my husband, my children, my precious grandbabies, my friends, my church, my future, all of the unknowns—for above all, He is faithful. At the heart of worship is God's love for us. He is present in this moment with you and with all His heart wants to know, "Do you know how much I love you?" Do you?

IN VIEW OF GOD'S MERCY

This chapter began with Paul's wonderful description of transforming worship in Romans 12:1-2. We worship by offering everything to God. Everything. Our relationships, our dreams, our service, our very being. So many heroes of our faith gave ultimate worship to God with their life.

Stephen would not be intimidated into silence by the religious bullies who charged him with disloyalty to God. He preached with such a sweet boldness. Just like his Savior, he forgave his persecutors as they killed him (see Acts 7:59-60).

The father of our faith, Abraham, offered back to God that which was most near and dear to his heart: his son, Isaac (see Genesis 22:1-10). What a terrifying Scripture passage. Can't you feel Abraham's agonizing obedience to trust God's love for him, even in losing his son—his long-awaited son of promise? But he worshiped, and God gave Isaac back to him (vv. 11-14).

For most of us reading the pages of this book, we live in relative safety when it comes to proclaiming the name of Jesus. But all over the world we have brothers and sisters who are paying the ultimate price—and experiencing the ultimate worship—of laying down their lives as martyrs for their unshakeable faith that God loves them. I recently heard the testimony of a precious mother who fled Mosul, Iraq—ISIS was going to make her sons fight their unholy war—and was now living in a refugee camp. "They took everything we had, but we have Jesus." Wow. The love of Christ is ultimately above and beyond anything we can possibly comprehend.

So remember, dear friends. True worship does not begin with what we offer to God, even if we lay down our very life. Do you see that tiny little phrase at the beginning of these verses in Romans 12:1? *"In view of God's mercy."* Spiritual worship and all that matters in life is because of, dependent upon, enabled by mercy. We offer our bodies as living sacrifices because we have experienced His amazing love.

The good news is that God gives us just what we need to live a life of worship. Jeremiah, the tenderhearted prophet, reminded people in captivity: "The faithful love of the Lord never ends! His mercies never cease. Great is his faithfulness; his mercies begin fresh each morning" (Lamentations 3:22-23). No matter what is going on in your life right now, look to God. Just like David, remember Him, put your hope in Him, praise Him, worship Him! Even if your emotions aren't feeling it. Even if you are tired or feeling numb. You can do it through an obedient act of your will.

As Evelyn Underhill taught:

God is acting on your soul all the time, whether you have spiritual sensations or not.[2] . . . The direction and constancy of the will is what really matters, and intellect and feelings are only important insofar as they contribute to that.[3]

In view of God's mercy—lavished upon you the moment you woke up this morning—offer Him yourself, your worship, and be transformed by a renewing of your mind.

AMAZING GRACE

Has any song touched more hearts and lives than "Amazing Grace"? The song begins with the unforgettable phrase, "Amazing grace, how sweet the sound, that saved a wretch like me."[4]

The wretch was, of course, John Newton, the man who penned the song. He went to sea with his father at age eleven. When his father died, nineteen-year-old John was forced into service on a British warship. He hated his life in the British navy and deserted, only to be captured and publicly flogged for his crime. He was demoted to the lowest level of service. But John Newton, angry and bitter, found a way to go even lower. He negotiated a transfer to work on a slave ship. His lot in life wasn't improved, as the captain abused him. But with a determined hatred, he rose through the ranks to the point he was made captain of his own ship—yes, he was a slaver.

On May 10, 1748—a day he would mark as his "new birthday" for the rest of his life—Newton's ship was caught in a ferocious storm. In a moment he could scarcely understand, he prayed for the first time in his life he could remember: "Lord, have mercy on us." Isn't it just like God to hear the prayer of a man whose life was cruel, without a hint of grace—truly wretched—and answer him?

Worship changes everything. It began with mercy for John Newton. The slaver went back to England, repented of his ways, and applied to be a minister. No surprise, he was turned down many times—his reputation preceded him. But through a hunger for God's Word, the encouragement of men like George Whitefield and John Wesley, and of course, amazing grace, John Newton persisted and became pastor in Olney, England. His preaching was so popular that the church had to be enlarged several times to accommodate the crowds. He preached and wrote hymns the rest of his life. He never forgot where he came from and was one of the founders and early leaders of the abolitionist movement.

That's amazing grace. That's worship. And it all began with mercy.

START HERE

I haven't sensed God's presence for a long time. I used to be so joyful. Now I feel like I'm going through the motions. I don't feel very loved or very loving.

Worship is based on God's worthiness and His presence—and His desire that we be present with Him. He wants us to experience Him and His goodness, His wonderful plans for our life. If you are struggling, my friend, please stop. *Don't try harder. Just trust more.* And what you need to trust in right now is God's love for you. Resting in the pure beauty of Jesus' love for us is quite confronting. How can this be? Surely there is *something* I can do to earn this favor?

But this is why the message of Christ is unlike any religion you'll ever hear about, for it is all about relationship. Maybe you don't think you deserve it. Good. That puts you one step closer to receiving it. For none of us deserve God's mercy. As Brennan Manning says in his book *The Ragamuffin Gospel,*

> We should be astonished at the goodness of God, stunned that He should bother to call us by name, our mouths wide open at His love, bewildered that at this very moment we are standing on holy ground.[5]

Tullian Tchividjian reminds us, "Legalism says God will love us if we change. The gospel says God will change us because He loves us."[6]

It's not by accident that the great evangelist Billy Graham would sing the song "Just As I Am," written by Charlotte Elliott in the nineteenth century, as he offered the gift of eternal life. The last verse is the beautiful cry of the heart of one who has discovered a love unknown:

> Just as I am—Thy love unknown
> Hath broken every barrier down;
> Now, to be Thine, yea Thine alone—
> O Lamb of God, I come, I come.[7]

David wrote the song of his life when he said, "My theme song is God's love and justice, and I'm singing it right to you, God" (Psalm 101:1 THE MESSAGE).

Have you discovered—truly discovered deep down—a love unknown? As God asks you, "Do you know how much I love you?" can you say from the bottom of your heart, "Yes"?

Talk to the Father. And never forget God is your Father! "See what great love the Father has lavished on us, that we should be called children of God! And that is what we are!" (1 John 3:1 NIV). Tell Him exactly where you are. Be totally honest. Ask Him to show you His love for you—and He will. I know this because I experience His love again and again, and it's this love that has changed everything.

CHAPTER 4

HIS LOVE FOR ME, MY LOVE FOR HIM

Love God, your God, with your whole heart: love him
with all that's in you, love him with all you've got!

DEUTERONOMY 6:5 THE MESSAGE

GOD'S WORD IS PURE BEAUTY AND POWER. Sometimes we discover truth through the laying down of principles, sometimes through songs and poems of praise and prayer, and sometimes through parables or stories. When God speaks through His Word, He brings to light the reality of who we are and our place in the world. He is always honest. He doesn't hide parts of His story and our story that are hard to hear and take.

Oh, what a story we find in the book of Hosea! From the way the book opens, we know we are in for quite a ride. We are going to face stark reality at its toughest. God tells Hosea, "Go and marry a prostitute, so that some of her children will be conceived in prostitution. This will illustrate how Israel has acted like a prostitute by turning against the Lord and worshiping other gods" (Hosea 1:2).

If you don't know this biblical writer, I can't suggest strongly enough that you get to know him. He ministered for sixty years in the northern kingdom of Israel—before and during the time the Assyrians conquered and scattered the ten "lost tribes." Some

49

call Hosea a "prophet of doom," but you can't read the entire book without discovering he was a man of brilliant hope, faith, and love. The book of Hosea is ultimately a love story, and a story of true worship—the kind of worship God desires from us.

A STORY OF GOD'S LOVE

Hosea's life is tragic, but it's also a beautiful picture of God's deep love for us. Hosea took a woman named Gomer—either a prostitute already or a woman who later became a prostitute—for his wife. They had children together. But whose children were they? She was not faithful to him. In his heartbreak and anger Hosea named their oldest child Jezreel—a valley where Israel had committed atrocities. He named their second child No-Mercy, and their third child Nobody (see The Message).

Now, that doesn't sound like the beginning of a love story, but stay with me. You see, God was fed up with His chosen people's infidelity. He wanted nothing more to do with them. Their actions were despicable, so he reminded Hosea of that by having him name his child after a place that represented their atrocities. Their loyalty was like vapor. They did not find their identity in the one who delivered them from slavery and gave them the Promised Land. So he had him name another child Nobody.

But we already know deep inside that's not the heart of God. That's not the final word. He wanted to shake the people out of their careless and casual disobedience; He wanted to wake them from their spiritual lethargy. But He could not—He would not—let them go. Worship is rooted in God's presence and begins for us in mercy: His unfailing mercy toward us.

God tells Hosea to rename not just his children, but each and every person in his country. They are to be called "God's Somebody" and "All Mercy" (Hosea 2:1 The Message). But God doesn't stop there. He tells Hosea to go find his wayward wife and to redeem her. Gomer had gotten herself into so much trouble that her lovers had sold her into slavery. Her husband bought her back.

How does Hosea approach his wife? With scorn and contempt? Does he treat her as she deserves? Not at all. He treats her with full love. He "allures" her, just as God allures us:

> "And now, here's what I'm going to do:
>> I'm going to start all over again.
> I'm taking her back out into the wilderness
>> where we had our first date, and I'll court her.
> I'll give her bouquets of roses.
>> I'll turn Heartbreak Valley into Acres of Hope.
> She'll respond like she did as a young girl, those days when
>> she was fresh out of Egypt."

Hosea 2:14-15 The Message

Now that's a love story! God allures us to Him.

OUR RESPONSE

What does God ask in return for His love? Hosea tells us—he shows us: "I'm after love that lasts, not more religion. I want you to know God, not go to more prayer meetings" (Hosea 6:6 The Message). *The Living Bible*, that wonderful paraphrase from the 1970s, puts it so eloquently: "I don't want your sacrifices—I want your love; I don't want your offerings—I want you to know me."

More than anything else, God wants our love. He wants us to fall as in love with Him as He is in love with us.

I will worship God all of my days, with all of my heart, with joy, praise, thanksgiving, and honor—not because He has told me He will punish me if I don't. I worship because of His amazing love that I experienced deep in my soul and that made me fall in love with Him.

I was the one who was lost. I was the slave in the marketplace. But when I accepted God's love for me, I truly caught a vision that I was God's beloved. I was beautiful. I was adored. I had a purpose. I was swept off my feet by a God who spoke "alluringly" right into my heart. How He saw me was all that mattered—not how others saw me or even how I saw myself. I fell in love with Jesus because of His love for me without borders or measure.

Worship changes everything. Why? It is rooted in our knowing in the very depth of our being how loved and cherished we are. We're not without mercy. We're not a nobody. We are God's Somebody.

Please don't miss this simple truth. Don't even read on if you don't know how much you are loved. You won't find anything deeper or more profound within the pages of this book. Fall in love with the one who created you, who knows you—every feeling, thought, and action—and loves you best. He's given you a name. You are Somebody—His Somebody. You are loved.

A RELATIONSHIP

The idea that worship is mostly about a Sunday service really misses the breadth that worship is in our lives. As we sing songs of praise, open His Word, gather together, and are refuelled for service—as wonderful as that is—it is just the beginning when it comes to the heart of worship. Did you notice what He told His chosen people through Hosea? "I don't want you to just show up for church and sing songs, give an offering, and bow your head for prayer. I want you to *know* me. I want you to *love* me."

Saint Augustine said, "To fall in love with God is the greatest of all romances; to seek Him, the greatest adventure; to find Him, the greatest human achievement."

A KING IN DISGUISE

The nineteenth-century philosopher Søren Kierkegaard wrote a parable to help us understand the incarnation—God coming to us in human form. It also explains how coming to us as a baby in the manger shows His desire for us to love Him freely:

Suppose there was a king who loved a humble maiden. The king was like no other king. Every statesman trembled before his power. No one dared breathe a word against him, for he had the strength to crush all opponents.

And yet this mighty king was melted by love for a humble maiden who lived in a poor village in his kingdom. How could he declare his love for her? In an odd sort of way, his kingliness tied his hands. If he brought her to the palace and crowned her head with jewels and clothed her body in royal robes, she would surely not resist—no one dared resist him. But would she love him?

She would say she loved him, of course, but would she truly? Or would she live with him in fear, nursing a private grief for the life she had left behind? Would she be happy at his side? How could he know for sure? If he rode to her forest cottage in his royal carriage, with an armed escort waving bright banners, that too would overwhelm her. He did not want a cringing subject. He wanted a lover, an equal. He wanted her to forget that he was a king and she a humble maiden and to let shared love cross the gulf between them. For it is only in love that the unequal can be made equal.

The king, convinced he could not elevate the maiden without crushing her freedom, resolved to descend to her. Clothed as a beggar, he approached her cottage with a worn cloak fluttering loose about him. It was no mere disguise, but a new identity he took on. He renounced the throne to win her hand.[1]

That's exactly what God did when He sent His Son to us. He told us, "I will not force you to love me. I want your love, but it must be freely given." The king is at your door. How will you respond?

Author and pastor Francis Chan puts the issue in front of us so we can't miss what is at stake: "The irony is that while God doesn't need us but still wants us, we desperately need God but don't really want Him most of the time."[2]

FALL IN LOVE

Don't just love God. *Fall in love with God.* In Psalm 18 we read of David's love for God. The whole Psalm reads like the plotline for a Hollywood blockbuster. It is a movie about a mighty king who leaves the comfort and splendor of his palace to rescue his beloved who is being held captive. David begins the psalm with the simple declaration: "I will love you, O Lord, my strength" (NKJV). I find it fascinating that David uses an expression of devotion—"I love you"—that wasn't in use in the Old Testament at this point. It might have felt too familiar to be applied to the Almighty—not enough reverence. But David couldn't hold back—he had to express what was in his heart!

If you haven't come to that point in your life journey, ask yourself what is holding you back. Is it a bad experience at church? I love my church and being at church. But just remember, we *are* His church. His body. And being a part of His expression on the earth is where I find my purpose and calling fulfilled in ways that are impossible outside of His church. But I know that many of us have also experienced hurt and disappointment in the very place God designed for us to feel loved and accepted. I can only say that people are imperfect. Not everyone who claims to speak for God truly echoes His words and heart. My gentle nudge is that you separate God's love from the sometimes imperfect love we show each other as humans—even as believers. If someone has harmed you in the name of God, please don't blame God for that. Bring that burden before God. Ask Him to show you His presence, His love, His heart for you. And now might be the time to forgive someone for wronging you. Don't let anyone rob you of knowing and experiencing God's love for you. Is it time for you to put your whole trust in God and not in others?

In His parable of the soils, Jesus warns His disciples and us: "Still others, like seed sown among thorns, hear the word; but the worries of this life, the deceitfulness of wealth and the desires for other things come in and choke the word, making it unfruitful"

(Mark 4:18-19 NIV). My friends, I would never deny you a single blessing from God. I stand as one who believes we *are* blessed, because of whose we are. But ultimately, what we most focus on is what we fall in love with. That's why Jesus said:

> "Sell your possessions and give to those in need. This will store up treasure for you in heaven! And the purses of heaven never get old or develop holes. Your treasure will be safe; no thief can steal it and no moth can destroy it. Wherever your treasure is, there the desires of your heart will also be."
>
> Luke 12:33-34

Don't let the fleeting pleasures and accumulation of this world rob you of loving the God who created you and owns "the cattle on a thousand hills" (Psalm 50:10) and all else that is of eternal value. Do you need to turn your eyes and heart back to God?

Is it because the people around you don't love and honor God and you've fallen into their patterns? Are you missing the spiritual encouragement of others who love God with all their hearts? Don't just *think* about finding a church—a fellowship of believers. Do it. Run there. Find that place. Jude was a humble slave who fell in love with Jesus. In his letter he reminds his brothers and sisters in Christ:

> But you, dear friends, must build each other up in your most holy faith, pray in the power of the Holy Spirit, and await the mercy of our Lord Jesus Christ, who will bring you eternal life. In this way, you will keep yourselves safe in God's love.
>
> Jude 1:20-21

Guard your heart toward God with those you are closest to. The writer to the Hebrews gives the same firm counsel:

> Let us hold unswervingly to the hope we profess, for he who promised is faithful. And let us consider how we may spur one another on toward love and good deeds, not giving

up meeting together, as some are in the habit of doing, but encouraging one another—and all the more as you see the Day approaching.

Hebrews 10:23-25 NIV

We need to walk through this world so that we can be salt and light to others. But just as surely, we need to keep our foot planted in the presence of those who will encourage us toward love and good deeds and the perfect will of God for our lives—to love God with our whole heart, soul, and mind.

Be very careful whom you allow to speak into your life when it comes to your love for God's house and His worth-ship. Jesus simplifies what is most important so powerfully in response to the question of a Pharisee who wanted to know what the most important commandment was. He said:

> "'Love the Lord your God with all your heart and with all your soul and with all your mind.' This is the first and greatest commandment. And the second is like it: 'Love your neighbor as yourself.' All the Law and the Prophets hang on these two commandments."

Matthew 22:37-40 NIV

Worship is knowing and loving God with all our heart, soul, strength, mind, and spirit. How could it be otherwise, knowing how much He loves us?

CHAPTER 5

MY PRAISE TO HIM

The Son is the image of the invisible God, the firstborn
over all creation. For in him all things were created:
things in heaven and on earth, visible and invisible,
whether thrones or powers or rulers or authorities; all things
have been created through him and for him. He is before
all things, and in him all things hold together.

COLOSSIANS 1:15-17 NIV

HE MUST BECOME GREATER

Near the beginning of Jesus' ministry, He and His followers met up with John the Baptist and his followers. It is quite probable that John was more famous and commanded bigger crowds than Jesus at the time. He was a stunning figure, wearing clothing made of camel hair and a big leather belt around his waist. His diet was honey and locusts. His message was bold and provocative: Repent! He was fearless. Later, it would cost him his life. He was mysterious, almost scary. But when John saw Jesus, his cousin, his spirit was moved:

> "Look, the Lamb of God, who takes away the sin of the world!
> This is the one I meant when I said, 'A man who comes after
> me has surpassed me because he was before me.' I myself did
> not know him, but the reason I came baptizing with water
> was that he might be revealed to Israel. . . .

57

"I saw the Spirit come down from heaven as a dove and remain on him. And I myself did not know him, but the one who sent me to baptize with water told me, 'The man on whom you see the Spirit come down and remain is the one who will baptize with the Holy Spirit.' I have seen and I testify that this is God's Chosen One."

John 1:29-34 NIV

John's words proclaimed God's greatness. John was a commanding figure, but he exalted the Great One. Despite such a powerful word of truth, his followers became jealous of Jesus' success and growing popularity. They complained to John: "Rabbi, that man who was with you on the other side of the Jordan—the one you testified about—look, he is baptizing, and everyone is going to him" (John 3:26 NIV).

John said, "Behold the Lamb of God." His followers referred to *that man*. They must have felt like baptism was for John alone—his trademark—not for someone new on the scene. What would you have done if you were John? It must break God's heart when we cling to our greatness, our position, our reputation, our achievements—even in ministry—and refuse to recognize who He is.

No, John didn't refer to Jesus as *that man*. He knew who Jesus was. In a beautiful teaching on humility and true worship, he declares:

"A person can receive only what is given them from heaven. You yourselves can testify that I said, 'I am not the Messiah but am sent ahead of him.' The bride belongs to the bridegroom. The friend who attends the bridegroom waits and listens for him, and is full of joy when he hears the bridegroom's voice. That joy is mine, and it is now complete. He must become greater; I must become less. The one who comes from above is above all; the one who is from the earth belongs to the earth, and speaks as one from the earth. The one who comes from heaven is above all."

John 3:27-31 NIV

He must become greater. I must become less. I must exalt Him. Because He is worthy. When I become less, and I proclaim Jesus as greater, a miracle begins to happen in my heart. I am changed.

FROM THE HEART

I will bless the Lord at all times: his praise shall continually be in my mouth. My soul shall make her boast in the Lord: the humble shall hear thereof, and be glad. O magnify the Lord with me, and let us exalt his name together.

Psalm 34:1-3 KJV

When some people hear the word *praise*, they shudder. I have heard from many people over the years who tell me they don't like praise; it's too confronting, too noisy. They will even come late to church on purpose to miss the "songs of praise." Isn't praise just a positive declaration of our words? Isn't praise simply something we joyfully express?

Yes and no, my friends. Let's ponder this a bit. If our words and actions flow from our heart, it is essential we understand what John the Baptist is teaching us. In essence, when he says "I must become less," he is not just referring to his ministry and personal impact, but to his very sense of being. Was he saying then that we should trim our sails and not feel so good about ourselves? Absolutely not. Follow John's story and you will not find a self-doubting, insecure man. Oh no. He is a bold, strong warrior to his dying day. He didn't beg and whimper for his life from Herod the tetrarch. He laid his neck on the line—literally—and declared truth.

John the Baptist is not calling for self-doubt and putting ourselves down; he is going beneath the surface and hitting at the root of what will block us from worship. He is attacking that old enemy of ours, pride. The pride that says, "I am king, I am lord of my life—not God."

If Satan can keep us distracted and clinging to our own personal lordship, he can keep us from true worship and praise.

He will dampen the joy that should permeate our praise. That's in keeping with his nature and story. He is ever the liar and deceiver. It's easy to forget that Satan (Lucifer, the Morning Star) was God's anointed angel. Gabriel was and is God's specially appointed messenger. Michael was and is God's great warrior angel—His sword, His enforcer. But both Gabriel and Michael were under the command of Lucifer. Lucifer's job was to bring the praise and worship of the angels before God himself. What did this beautifully created, much loved creature do? Out of pride and personal glory, he claimed for himself what was God's. He wanted the praise.

His just reward was to be cast out from heaven. Since the day he stopped praising God, there is nothing he desires more than stealing the glory that is God's, and he does that when he turns our eyes from God's glory to self-glory, from God worship to self-worship, from joyful praise to muted, lifeless praise. That's much different from God's desire that we love ourselves as He loves us. That's much different from bold confidence in the abilities and gifts God has granted us.

I am convinced that Satan was putting John the Baptist to the test in this poignant encounter with Jesus. I believe Satan wanted him to agree with his followers and say, "Wait a minute. I'm the man. I'm in charge!"

I am convinced that Satan will attack us the same way. There is no better way to turn positive, joyful, contagious, enthusiastic praise among God's people—even His anointed ministers—than by convincing them that they are worthy of praise.

No, we will never say it like that. But as we delve into our first response of worship, just know that praise is not only our words, but the set of our heart. Praise goes beyond—and deeper—than recognizing and saying that He is worthy. It is an affirmation in our heart and every fiber of our being. Praise is our stance of faith. Praise is a weapon. Praise announces God's reign in our hearts.

Praise and worship are such a joy. But they also wage war on the battleground at the deepest levels of our existence. It is a question of lordship.

He must become greater. I must become less. I must exalt Him. Because He is worthy. When I become less—and I proclaim Jesus as greater—a miracle begins to happen in my heart. I am changed. Everything changes because He is Lord!

THE GLORY OF THE LORD

We often think of glory as something mysterious, but the clearest definition of glory is "weight." Glory refers to something real and substantial. His greatness. Isaiah tells us that when the glory of the Lord is revealed, it turns the world upside down!

> Fill in the valleys, and level the mountains and hills.
> Straighten the curves, and smooth out the rough places.
> Then the glory of the Lord will be revealed, and all people
> will see it together. The Lord has spoken!
>
> Isaiah 40:4-5

When we exalt the one who is worthy, nothing is as it was before; not even valleys and mountains are the same. We delight in the fact that we are not the Creator but the created. Our lives aren't diminished, because when we lift up the glory of God, we receive life-changing joy. We reflect that glory as it shines on us and seeps into us. God's glory is His beauty, His splendor, His strength, His magnificence. Nothing I am or have compares. I want to reflect Him.

After leaving slavery in Egypt for the Promised Land, the people were so terrified of God that they refused to go on the mountain to see Him. They told Moses to go in their place so they wouldn't die in His overwhelming presence. Often they may have had fickle and stubborn hearts, but at this moment they weren't all wrong.

When speaking directly to God, Moses said, "Now show me your glory" (Exodus 33:18 NIV). God responded to this bold worshiper:

"I will cause my goodness to pass in front of you, and I will proclaim my name, the Lord, in your presence. I will have mercy on whom I will have mercy, and I will have compassion on whom I will have compassion. But," he said, "you cannot see my face, for no one may see me and live."

Exodus 33:19-20 NIV

So powerful, so substantial was the glory of God that He offered Moses a way to behold Him without dying:

The Lord continued, "Look, stand near me on this rock. As my glorious presence passes by, I will hide you in the crevice of the rock and cover you with my hand until I have passed by. Then I will remove my hand and let you see me from behind. But my face will not be seen."

Exodus 33:21-23

How do we behold and proclaim a glory that might kill us? Here's the lesson: Seek all of the glory of God He will reveal to you—all that you are ready to see. Psalm 91:1 encourages us again to draw near to God: "He who dwells in the secret place of the Most High shall abide under the shadow of the Almighty" (NKJV). Yes, we can always trust in His glory, which longs to cover and protect us.

THE COST OF WORSHIP

What will worship cost you? For us to worship Jesus Christ freely, it cost *Him* everything. Magnifying God, declaring His greatness, His worthiness, is exactly what Jesus showed us in the garden on the night before His crucifixion. He knew what was coming: the torture of body and soul. So deep was His knowledge of the coming agony that He sweated blood. He was all human and felt the same pains we feel. But He declared His Father's glory in the most powerful prayer ever recorded: "Father, if you are willing, please take this cup of suffering away from me. Yet I want your will to be done, not mine" (Luke 22:42).

We relate to King David so well because we feel the same things he expressed throughout the Psalms: joy, discouragement, anger, relief, thankfulness, fear, self-pity, hope, and so much more. We know the accounts of his failures, particularly his relationship with Bathsheba and how he covered it up with murder. We find hope for our own failures as he received forgiveness and restoration.

But one of David's failings is not quite so well known. In a moment of pride, he had a census taken of Israel (see 2 Samuel 24). This displeased God. Why? God sees into the hearts of people—and into the heart of His anointed one. The king and his court were counting people to figure out how great they had become. Wow—look at what we have accomplished. Let's see just how far we've come. They were moving from trust in God—from exalting Him—to self-reliance, to proclaiming their own worth and savvy. God pierced David's heart with conviction, and David knew what he had done and was doing. He didn't argue. Rather, he repented in the face of God's anger. He took full responsibility.

> When David saw the angel, he said to the Lord, "I am the one who has sinned and done wrong! But these people are as innocent as sheep—what have they done? Let your anger fall against me and my family."
>
> **2 Samuel 24:17**

As a reminder of the folly of pride, God directed David to build an altar. David took his men to build it. The spot he selected was the threshing floor of Araunah. When Araunah heard that David wanted to purchase the threshing floor, he quickly offered it as a gift to his king:

> "Take it, my lord the king, and use it as you wish," Araunah said to David. "Here are oxen for the burnt offering, and you

can use the threshing boards and ox yokes for wood to build
a fire on the altar."

2 Samuel 24:22

Araunah was obviously a politically wise man! Get on the
good side of the king with a gift. But what was David's response?
He refused the offer. "No, I insist on buying it, for I will not present
burnt offerings to the Lord my God that have cost me nothing"
(v. 24).

What is the cost of worship? It is our everything. We give ourselves totally and completely as living sacrifices. We pray "not my
will, but Yours." We say, "He must become greater, I must become
less important." We acknowledge that He is the Creator and we are
the created.

THE JOY OF PRAISE

When David reestablished worship with the Ark of the Covenant—
the physical representation of God's presence—he sang a song
that is not recorded in the Psalms:

> Give thanks to the Lord and proclaim his greatness.
>> Let the whole world know what he has done.
> Sing to him; yes, sing his praises.
>> Tell everyone about his wonderful deeds.
> Exult in his holy name;
>> rejoice, you who worship the Lord.
> Search for the Lord and for his strength;
>> continually seek him.
> Remember the wonders he has performed,
>> his miracles, and the rulings he has given,
> you children of his servant Israel,
>> you descendants of Jacob, his chosen ones.
>
> He is the Lord our God.
>> His justice is seen throughout the land.
> Remember his covenant forever—

the commitment he made to a thousand generations.
This is the covenant he made with Abraham
    and the oath he swore to Isaac.
He confirmed it to Jacob as a decree,
    and to the people of Israel as a never-ending covenant:
"I will give you the land of Canaan
    as your special possession."
He said this when you were few in number,
    a tiny group of strangers in Canaan.
They wandered from nation to nation,
    from one kingdom to another.
Yet he did not let anyone oppress them.
    He warned kings on their behalf:
"Do not touch my chosen people,
    and do not hurt my prophets."

Let the whole earth sing to the Lord!
    Each day proclaim the good news that he saves.
Publish his glorious deeds among the nations.
    Tell everyone about the amazing things he does.
Great is the Lord! He is most worthy of praise!
    He is to be feared above all gods.
The gods of other nations are mere idols,
    but the Lord made the heavens!
Honor and majesty surround him;
    strength and joy fill his dwelling.

O nations of the world, recognize the Lord,
    recognize that the Lord is glorious and strong.
Give to the Lord the glory he deserves!
    Bring your offering and come into his presence.
Worship the Lord in all his holy splendor.
    Let all the earth tremble before him.
    The world stands firm and cannot be shaken.

Let the heavens be glad, and the earth rejoice!
    Tell all the nations, "The Lord reigns!"
Let the sea and everything in it shout his praise!

Let the fields and their crops burst out with joy!
Let the trees of the forest sing for joy before the Lord,
   for he is coming to judge the earth.
Give thanks to the Lord, for he is good!
   His faithful love endures forever.
Cry out, "Save us, O God of our salvation!
   Gather and rescue us from among the nations,
so we can thank your holy name
   and rejoice and praise you."
Praise the Lord, the God of Israel,
   who lives from everlasting to everlasting!

1 Chronicles 16:8-36

David reaffirmed what was in his heart: God's greatness. He deserves all our praise. He is worthy. Something wonderful happens when we give all glory to God. We receive His gladness. May we never forget that truth. His glory, proclaimed from our hearts and lips, brings our gladness. His joy in our lives equals strength.

When we give ourselves to God, we lose nothing of value. We receive gifts beyond measure. The martyred missionary Jim Elliot said it so profoundly: "He is no fool who gives what he cannot keep to gain what he cannot lose."[1]

Praise brings us gladness. Evangelist Jonathan Edwards said, "The happiness of the creature consists in rejoicing in God, by which also God is magnified and exalted."[2] At the same time, our praise brings God gladness. John Piper says, "The climax of God's happiness is the delight He takes in the echoes of His excellence in the praises of His people."[3] Rick Warren adds, "Every human activity, except sin, can be done for God's pleasure, if you do it with an attitude of praise."[4]

That's worship!

66

HOW TO PRAISE

We exalt God in what we believe in our heart. But never forget that we exalt God with our words! Our words must express the honor and respect and love we feel for God inside us. That's why David tells us to sing, to proclaim, to shout, to cry out, to praise.

Paul warns us to avoid the wrong kinds of words: "Let there be no filthiness (obscenity, indecency) nor foolish and sinful (silly and corrupt) talk, nor coarse jesting, which are not fitting or becoming; but instead voice your thankfulness [to God]" (Ephesians 5:4 Amplified).

Note that he says to *voice* your thankfulness. Later in that chapter he says,

> Therefore do not be vague and thoughtless and foolish, but understanding and firmly grasping what the will of the Lord is. And do not get drunk with wine, for that is debauchery; but ever be filled and stimulated with the [Holy] Spirit. Speak out to one another in psalms and hymns and spiritual songs, offering praise with voices [and instruments] and making melody with all your heart to the Lord.
>
> VV. 17–19 Amplified

Did you catch the need for us to express our words out loud? *"Speak out to one another . . . offering praise with voices!"*

Perhaps the simplest and clearest teaching on how to praise is found in Psalm 50. This beautiful passage is just six short verses—but the word *praise* is found thirteen times!

In verse one we discover where to worship: in His sanctuary and under His heavens. In other words, everywhere!

In verse two we discover why we are to praise Him: for His mighty works and His greatness. We praise Him for who He is and all He has done!

In verses four through six we discover ways we are to praise Him: with a ram's horn, a lyre, a harp, tambourines, strings, flutes, and loud clanging symbols. We are to praise Him with everything that has breath. When we worship at church, it is passionate. We shout. We go for it with everything we've got. For anyone not comfortable with this kind of expression, I would just direct their attention back to Psalm 50. Worship changes everything. It happens anywhere and everywhere we acknowledge God's presence, for truly He is everywhere. Worship happens when we realize how much God loves us and respond to Him with our love and devotion and honor Him with our praise.

May I gently ask you: Whom are you exalting? False humility tries to veil pride in actions that again draw attention to ourselves. I pray that we will be more like John the Baptist, who fully realized that there was "one coming who is greater than me" (see John 1:15).

I wonder why you care, God—
   why do you bother with us at all?
All we are is a puff of air;
   we're like shadows in a campfire.

Step down out of heaven, God;
   ignite volcanoes in the hearts of the mountains.
Hurl your lightnings in every direction;
   shoot your arrows this way and that.
Reach all the way from sky to sea:
   pull me out of the ocean of hate,
   out of the grip of those barbarians
Who lie through their teeth,
   who shake your hand
   then knife you in the back.

O God, let me sing a new song to you.

PSALM 144:3-9

CHAPTER 6

MY GRATITUDE TO HIM

*Enter his gates with thanksgiving; go into his courts
with praise. Give thanks to him and praise his name.*

PSALM 100:4

JESUS INVITED TEN MEN to a worship service. They didn't have to drive or get a ride. Jesus just showed up where they were. Imagine that. Being in the presence of our Savior. And this wasn't just any worship service. Ten men were invited, all ten were suffering from a debilitating illness, and all ten men were healed. Wow! Wouldn't you want to be there?

But sadly, only one experienced true worship. Only one fell at the feet of Jesus and then rose to dance with joy. Ten left, thrilled to be healed, but only one returned to experience deeper levels of being in the presence of Jesus Christ. What brought him back? Gratitude. He came back to say thank you to God, the Creator, the Healer, the Giver of all good gifts. Jesus' response is amazement at how few received the totality of His offer.

> One of them, when he realized that he was healed, came back to Jesus, shouting, "Praise God!" He fell to the ground at Jesus' feet, thanking him for what he had done. This man was a Samaritan. Jesus asked, "Didn't I heal ten men? Where are the other nine? Has no one returned to give glory to God except

this foreigner?" And Jesus said to the man, "Stand up and go. Your faith has healed you."

Luke 17:15-20

Worship always begins by faith. But it becomes a life-changing force in every area and moment of our lives through thanksgiving.

My friends, nothing will change our attitudes, our relationships, our circumstances like thanksgiving. Gratitude is when you realize how blessed and rich you are in Christ. In one of David's most beautiful psalms of worship, he tells us to make a joyful noise unto the Lord, but it's no accident that He includes the powerful phrase "Enter His gates with thanksgiving"! Psalm 100 shows just how entwined thanksgiving and worship are.

> Shout with joy to the Lord, all the earth!
> Worship the Lord with gladness.
> Come before him, singing with joy.
> Acknowledge that the Lord is God!
> He made us, and we are his.
> We are his people, the sheep of his pasture.
> Enter his gates with thanksgiving;
> go into his courts with praise.
> Give thanks to him and praise his name.
> For the Lord is good.
> His unfailing love continues forever,
> and his faithfulness continues to each generation.

SO BLESSED

Gratitude is when we recognize that everything we have and are comes from the hand of God. It is that moment when we realize how blessed we truly are. It is the pathway to joy. We no longer focus on petty grievances and hurts, knowing how forgiven we are. We stop comparing the size of our house and bank account to others, wondering why we don't have more. Why would we ever feel like we have been short-changed knowing that we have been given all the riches and treasures of God inside us? Oh how it must break His heart when He lavishes himself on His children and we forget to express thanksgiving.

If you read through Proverbs you will find countless warnings against the pride that says "I am self-made and self-sufficient." Proverbs 16 is filled with reminders to realize God is the source of wisdom and blessing and success:

> Mortals make elaborate plans,
>> but God has the last word. . . .
> We plan the way we want to live,
>> but only God makes us able to live it. . . .
> First pride, then the crash—
>> the bigger the ego, the harder the fall. . . .
> Make your motions and cast your votes,
>> but God has the final say.
>
> Proverbs 16:1, 9, 18, 33 THE MESSAGE

KING OF THE WORLD

Nebuchadnezzar, King of Babylon, was one of the most successful and powerful men that ever lived. He was fascinated with God's people, whom his nation had made captive. The more he watched and listened, the more he began to recognize that there was one true God who brought all blessings. The persistent, joyful commitment of God's people awakened his spiritual life. He wanted more. He was ready to worship!

But in a poignant life moment, he went to the highest point in his palace, looked down on his kingdom, and declared: "Look at this, Babylon the great! And I built it all by myself, a royal palace adequate to display my honor and glory!" (Daniel 4:30 THE MESSAGE). What happened next is a personal spiritual tragedy. He surrendered his spark of faith in the one true God to the delusion that he was god, that he was the one in charge of his life and realm. It was all downhill from there. He fell into a depression and a mental disorder in which he descended into living as a beast:

The words were no sooner out of his mouth than a voice out of heaven spoke, "This is the verdict on you, King Nebuchadnezzar: Your kingdom is taken from you. You will be driven out of human company and live with the wild animals. You will eat grass like an ox. The sentence is for seven seasons, enough time to learn that the High God rules human kingdoms and puts whomever he wishes in charge."

It happened at once. Nebuchadnezzar was driven out of human company, ate grass like an ox, and was soaked in heaven's dew. His hair grew like the feathers of an eagle and his nails like the claws of a hawk.

Daniel 4:31-33 THE MESSAGE

We don't have to rule a kingdom to believe we are a god. Isn't that ultimately what the sin of pride is? *I am in control, not God.*

Nothing will sabotage our spiritual vigor, our contagious joy, than to lose our sense of gratitude. Thanksgiving is an acknowledgment of Psalm 100:3: "Know this: God is God, and God, God. He made us; we didn't make him. We're his people, his well-tended sheep" (THE MESSAGE).

We worship because God is worthy of our worship. It begins with His presence and takes root in our lives because of his magnificent love. We respond in faith with love and praise . . . and thanksgiving!

GIVING GOD CREDIT FOR WHAT HE HAS DONE

I will say this many times throughout the book: *Words are so powerful.* They curse and they bless. Ask yourself this: Do my words express thanksgiving to God for all He has given me and all He is in my life—or do my words declare *my* power, *my* goodness, *my* abilities, *my* accomplishments? Am I giving myself credit for what God has done for me?

One set of words—words of self-exaltation—is a slippery slope to defeat. But when our words acknowledge the goodness of God and express thanksgiving to Him, when we return with the leper to the presence of Jesus Christ, we experience worship that brings life and joy.

I can't stress this enough. A thankful heart will affect your co-workers, neighbors, friends, family, children, and spouse as your spirit of gratitude spills over, building friendship and community. Your words bring healing and express love because you are no longer pushing yourself on others, but sharing the loving-kindness of God.

The world doesn't need our brilliant arguments. The world is dying to see us acknowledge in our attitudes and words the love of God. That only happens when everything we do and say is seasoned with thanksgiving to God.

PREPARE YOUR HEART

When I am leading worship, I do my very best to prepare musically. I plan and I rehearse. I want to offer back to God the gifts He has given to me as best as I possibly can. I also practice and rehearse so that my mind and spirit are free to follow God's leading. I don't want to worry about notes and rhythm and words and not be free to participate in and experience true worship in my own life. But no preparation is more important than time in God's presence. I want to lift up Jesus. I don't want to exalt gifts that God has given me. I want to exalt the Giver. So my prayers are seasoned with thanksgiving. Thank you, God, for using me. Thank you, God, for trusting me with this opportunity to experience your presence. Thank you, God, for allowing me to lead others as we release worship by the power of the Holy Spirit.

When you feel discontent, when you struggle to evidence the fruit of the Spirit, when you are jealous of others, when you feel you have been cheated in life, when you feel resentments and grievances easily, when relationships are rocky, when God feels distant and you have little desire to be in His presence and with His people—first ask yourself about your heart and words. Are you a person of gratitude? Even if the embers of gratitude are burning low in your heart, fan them back to flame by your words. Speak gratitude. Often. *Thank you. Thank you. Thank you.* Speak the words to the best of your ability until you feel them in your heart. Don't just speak them at church or before a meal. Speak them everywhere.

I love what the nineteenth-century British author G. K. Chesterton said:

> You say grace before meals. All right. But I say grace before the play and the opera, and grace before the concert and pantomime, and grace before I open a book, and grace before sketching, painting, swimming, fencing, boxing, walking, playing, dancing; and grace before I dip the pen in the ink.[1]

We thank God in all circumstances!

We don't worship God—or thank God—for what we will get in return. But Charles Spurgeon hits the nail on the head when he says, "It is not how much we have, but how much we enjoy, that makes happiness."[2]

Our God is so gracious. Our very response of thanksgiving to what He has given us means He gives us even more!

IN ALL THINGS

David's words are packed with his heart and spirit. They become so powerful that we can almost feel exactly what he is going through, even his pain.

> O Lord, don't rebuke me in your anger
>   or discipline me in your rage.
> Have compassion on me, Lord, for I am weak.
>   Heal me, Lord, for my bones are in agony.
> I am sick at heart.
> How long, O Lord, until you restore me?
>
> Return, O Lord, and rescue me.
>   Save me because of your unfailing love.

For the dead do not remember you.
Who can praise you from the grave?

I am worn out from sobbing.
All night I flood my bed with weeping,
drenching it with my tears.
My vision is blurred by grief;
my eyes are worn out because of all my enemies.

Psalm 6:1-7

His bones ache. His heart is sick. He has nearly passed out and can barely see what is right in from of him through his river of tears. But even as he pleads with God to rescue him, he shows his true heart of gratitude when he asks, "Who can thank you from the grave?" (see NKJV).

Even facing death, even filled with pain, even when life wasn't following the exact plan he had in mind, even when feeling sorry for himself, David's heart still resounded with thanksgiving. Is it any wonder he was such a wonderful leader of worship? He knew his relationship with God.

Paul puts it so simply and beautifully when he tells us: "Rejoice always, pray continually, give thanks in all circumstances; for this is God's will for you in Christ Jesus" (1 Thessalonians 5:16-18 NIV). Eugene Peterson translates this in *The Message*: "Be cheerful no matter what; pray all the time; thank God no matter what happens. This is the way God wants you who belong to Christ Jesus to live."

All circumstances. No matter what. All the time. Continually.

When Daniel learned that men were plotting evil against him, "he got down on his knees and prayed, giving thanks to his God, just as he had done before" (Daniel 6:10 NIV). *"Just as he had done before . . ."* They wanted to kill him! That's not the time to be thankful, is it? That's exactly the time we need to express gratitude. Circumstances didn't matter to Daniel—thanksgiving was part of his life. Is it any wonder he came out of the lions' den unscratched?

Thanksgiving is an important aspect of worship. And like worship, it is not to be set aside for certain moments—morning devotions, Sunday morning worship, sitting at the table for dinner, when everything is going our way—but for every moment, every place, and every circumstance of life.

We don't always see or know how God is working in our lives and blessing us all the time. That is our own ignorance and limitation. But when we thank God in all circumstances—even the hard ones, even when we are not sure what He is bringing forth in our lives, but knowing full well He is on our side and has our back—then our eyes are opened to His work. Just as the flooded Jordan River didn't part for Joshua until he put a foot in the swollen, rushing stream (see Joshua 3), God is calling us to step out with intentional obedience and express thanks to Him. The Holy Spirit will give you the ability to be thankful, even in your darkest hour.

Love draws us close to God with the bonds of relationship. Praise is honoring God for who He is. Thanksgiving is thanking God for what He has done. Love, praise, and thanksgiving make up the heart of our part in worship. They are our faithful responses to His worthiness, His presence, and His love. They are the expressions of our faith, the gift that God has put in our being that allows us by His grace and spirit to respond to Him at all.

Warren Wiersbe says, "Worship is the believer's response of all that they are—mind, emotions, will, body—to what God is and says and does."[3] A. W. Tozer says, "We must never rest until everything inside us worships God."[4]

God is worthy of our worship. He desires us to freely love Him. We have so much to thank Him for.

Sing the song. Tell the story of what He has done for you. Come back into the presence of Jesus—the one who has healed and restored your soul—jumping and shouting and saying "Thank you!"

THE HANDS OF

PART TWO

Worship

Therefore, I urge you, brothers and sisters, in view of God's mercy, to offer your bodies as a living sacrifice, holy and pleasing to God—this is your true and proper worship.

ROMANS 12:1 NIV

As we worship God in and through the relationships, activities, and places in our lives, His power changes us.

CHAPTER 7

MY SERVICE

For we are God's masterpiece.
He has created us anew in Christ Jesus,
so we can do the good things
he planned for us long ago.

EPHESIANS 2:10

DEAR GOD, USE ME TODAY. That's my simple prayer each morning. May my eyes be awake and aware to all He would have me put my hand to. I have experienced His amazing grace in my life time and time again. When I accepted Christ into my life, I discovered I was a masterpiece—created anew in Christ Jesus—and able to serve and minister in ways that God had planned for me before I was even born! I was amazed that one of my first responses as a Christian was to *serve*.

And this is why I respond in worship. When we move from *doing* worship to *being in* worship, a wondrous flow of grace moves in and out of us as naturally as breathing. Service is no longer an effort, but something that happens without our seeming to try. But I don't want you to miss something very important. We don't worship and then serve as two distinct activities of life. Serving *is* worshiping. Breathing includes both inhaling and exhaling as a single function of the body; in the same way, worship includes receiving and giving.

In Romans 12:1, a passage we refer to several times in this book, Paul explicitly ties together worship and serving: we offer our bodies—all that we are—as an act of spirit-worship. He urges and pleads with us to respond to God's mercy with service: "I urge you, brothers and sisters, in view of God's mercy, to offer your bodies as a living sacrifice, holy and pleasing to God—this is your true and proper worship" (NIV).

The Greek word *latreuo* is translated as "worship" three times in the Word. In Acts 24:14, Paul explains to the ruler that he worships (latreuo) just as his ancestors did. It actually means to minister to God, to render religious homage, to do the service, to worship.

LOVING OTHERS

The heart of service is loving others. That's why Jesus summarizes all the laws and requirements of God as loving Him with all our might and loving others as we love ourselves. This shines a bright light on one of the encounters Jesus had with Peter. He had already called Peter "the rock" and declared that his spiritual recognition of Jesus as Messiah was the foundation of our church testimony (see Matthew 16:16-18). But Peter was far from perfect. When given the opportunity to pray with Jesus in His moment of anguish, Peter slept (see Mark 14:32-37). When Peter had the opportunity to declare his allegiance with Jesus, he denied Him three times (see Mark 14:66-72). While the women went to the tomb to anoint Jesus' body, Peter hid behind shuttered windows (see John 20:19).

No wonder the resurrected Christ wanted to make sure Peter knew his place in the kingdom. In a setting that seems somewhat familiar—after all, Jesus called Peter to leave his boat and become a fisher of men the first time they spoke—He again calls him to leave his boat and come to shore, but only after helping him haul in one of the biggest fishing catches of his life (see John 21:1-6). When Peter recognizes Jesus and hears His voice calling him ashore, he does what Peter does. He dives in head-first.

Then the disciple Jesus loved said to Peter, "It's the Master!" When Simon Peter realized that it was the Master, he threw on some clothes, for he was stripped for work, and dove into the sea. The other disciples came in by boat for they weren't far from land, a hundred yards or so, pulling along the net full of fish. When they got out of the boat, they saw a fire laid, with fish and bread cooking on it.

John 21:7-9 The Message

After Jesus sends Peter back to the boat to help the others haul in their tremendous catch, and then feeds Peter and six other disciples breakfast, he pulls Peter aside for a serious conversation, a conversation about service and love.

After breakfast, Jesus said to Simon Peter, "Simon, son of John, do you love me more than these?"

"Yes, Master, you know I love you."

Jesus said, "Feed my lambs."

He then asked a second time, "Simon, son of John, do you love me?"

"Yes, Master, you know I love you."

Jesus said, "Shepherd my sheep."

Then he said it a third time: "Simon, son of John, do you love me?"

Peter was upset that he asked for the third time, "Do you love me?" so he answered, "Master, you know everything there is to know. You've got to know that I love you."

Jesus said, "Feed my sheep. I'm telling you the very truth now: When you were young you dressed yourself and went wherever you wished, but when you get old you'll have to stretch out your hands while someone else dresses you and takes you where you don't want to go." He said this to hint at the kind of death by which Peter would glorify God. And then he commanded, "Follow me."

John 21:15-18 The Message

The reality of Peter's failures had to be faced. The cost of following Jesus had to be seen for what it was: *everything.* But why ask Peter three times if he loved Jesus? The first two times Peter answered, he used the word that can be translated "like." In other words, "I love you as a good friend." Jesus wanted more. The third time he asked Peter if he loved Him, Peter finally answered with the word *agape*. "I love you unconditionally, all in, with everything I've got and am."

Jesus no longer had to tell him, "Feed my sheep." For when we love our Savior unconditionally, wholeheartedly, with all worship and adoration, He knows we will feed His sheep; He knows we will serve others as an outflow of our worship.

WORSHIP IS EVERYTHING

The first part of this book covered the heart of worship: from *He is worthy* to *I am thankful*; from God's burning desire for us to have relationship with Him to my affirmation of "Yes, Lord, yes"; from His incredible love for me to my falling in love with Him. But just as serving is worship, all that follows becomes the exhaling of the breath of love God breathed into us. What that means is that not only does worship change everything, but worship is everything we do and are.

Somehow we have picked up the notion that we worship at church and then go and serve in the world as a separate activity. The deep Christian apologist Ravi Zacharias put it this way: "For the Christian, worship is coextensive with life. Life is already an expression of worship."[1] We might come to that realization at different times and in different ways in our walk with God. But the connection will click in your heart and mind through service that is empowered by the Holy Spirit and inspired by God's love in your life.

Rick Warren says, "After learning to love God (worship), learning to love others is the second purpose of your life."[2] I agree wholeheartedly with him, but would humbly add: Both purposes, both commands, both activities are designed by God to happen together, as natural spiritual breathing. When your worship is in awe of the Father, in love with Jesus, and in step with the Spirit, it will overflow with service as an active love for the world—even loving your enemies—and it will transform every area of your life completely.

TRUE GREATNESS

The mother of James and John came to Jesus with a request. "In your Kingdom, please let my two sons sit in places of honor next to you, one on your right and the other on your left" (Matthew 20:21). It was good that she wanted her sons to be as close to Jesus as possible. But unfortunately, her understanding of the nature of God's kingdom was based on a worldly understanding of greatness. Her request was not spiritual but rather political. The other followers saw what she was trying to do and grumbled at her audacity. But for the wrong reason. They were just as misguided about greatness as this mother.

Later, after returning to the garden of Gethsemane, these same disciples were offered places at Jesus' right and left. "My soul is crushed with grief to the point of death. Stay here and keep watch with me" (Mark 14:34). They slept. Perhaps if they truly wanted to be at Jesus' left and right side, they would have hung on crosses next to Him, in place of the two criminals.

Jesus was saying, "If you want to be great . . . give." He was teaching them and us that the closer we draw to Jesus in love and worship, the more that closeness, that experience of God's presence, will show up in service. Billy Graham spoke this truth so powerfully when he said, "The highest form of worship is the worship of unselfish Christian service. The greatest form of praise is the sound of consecrated feet seeking out the lost and helpless."[3]

THE HEART OF GOD

The Father sent the Son into the world to seek and save the lost. We have been redeemed by the blood of Jesus to become worshipers.

And as worshipers, we are to reflect the heart of our Redeemer. What is the heart of Jesus? He tells us,

> "Whoever wants to be great must become a servant. Whoever wants to be first among you must be your slave. That is what the Son of Man has done: He came to serve, not to be served— and then to give away his life in exchange for many who are held hostage."
>
> **Mark 10:45** THE MESSAGE

He asks us to follow Him and serve with the same love and passion He has: "Anyone who holds on to life just as it is destroys that life. But if you let it go, reckless in your love, you'll have it forever, real and eternal" (John 12:25 THE MESSAGE).

This is not a new legalism. It is not a return to salvation through works. The writer to the Hebrews reminds us,

> If that animal blood and the other rituals of purification were effective in cleaning up certain matters of our religion and behavior, think how much more the blood of Christ cleans up our whole lives, inside and out. Through the Spirit, Christ offered himself as an unblemished sacrifice, freeing us from all those dead-end efforts to make ourselves respectable, so that we can live all out for God.
>
> **Hebrews 9:13-15** THE MESSAGE

God loves to share His love through followers who are sold out to worshiping and serving Him. This reflects what He said to the people of Israel through the prophets:

> "They will be my people," says the Lord of Heaven's Armies. "On the day when I act in judgment, they will be my own special treasure. I will spare them as a father spares an obedient child. Then you will again see the difference between the righteous and the wicked, between those who serve God and those who do not."
>
> **Malachi 3:17-18**

I love the words of Jesus in Matthew 25. He tells the story of those who showed deep love and devotion for a king. The king thanked them for their faithful, loving service to him, but they looked at each other in confusion.

> "Lord, when did we ever see you hungry and feed you? Or thirsty and give you something to drink? Or a stranger and show you hospitality? Or naked and give you clothing? When did we ever see you sick or in prison and visit you?"
>
> And the King will say, "I tell you the truth, when you did it to one of the least of these my brothers and sisters, you were doing it to me!"
>
> Matthew 25:37-40

Our ministry, our compassion, and our kindness to others is kindness to God. It is worship.

STRENGTH TO SERVE

If in serving others you feel drained of all strength and have lost the joy of salvation, I would simply say that you must always keep your eyes on Jesus rather than on the task at hand. Otherwise you'll end up trying to serve or earn your way into heaven to avoid hell. Jesus loves us and takes us as we are, and all we need to do is come back to the wonderful realization that we are saved before attempting anything for God. Your gracious heavenly Father has called you His child out of His great mercy. There is nothing you can do to earn His love—not even serving others. Our motivation can never be to make ourselves acceptable to God.

In Psalm 51, where David comes to God for forgiveness, he hits the motivation of our deeds head on. If he could cleanse himself, he would. But he knows only God can wash his filthy clothing of sin whiter than snow. What of his sacrifice and service to God?

You do not desire a sacrifice, or I would offer one.
    You do not want a burnt offering.
The sacrifice you desire is a broken spirit.
    You will not reject a broken and repentant heart, O God.
Look with favor on Zion and help her;
    rebuild the walls of Jerusalem.
Then you will be pleased with sacrifices offered in the right
        spirit—
    with burnt offerings and whole burnt offerings.
    Then bulls will again be sacrificed on your altar.

Psalm 51:16-19

Get connected and let Him breathe into your being all the joy and strength you need to do His will.

Service is not a tedious chore but a delight. In fact, in His presence we find fullness of joy and strength that defies all odds! Do you feel you are facing a mountain? Then expect a mountain of grace and strength. The nineteenth-century American pastor Phillips Brooks said this:

> Do not pray for easy lives. Pray to be stronger men! Do not pray for tasks equal to your powers. Pray for powers equal to your tasks! Then the doing of your work shall be no miracle, but you shall be the miracle.[4]

Charles Spurgeon's insight on having the strength we need to serve is incredible:

> Once more, observe, that in the service of God strength will always be given according to your day. When you serve the Lord, if He sends you out upon a tough piece of work, He will give you extra Grace. And if He calls you to great suffering, He will give you greater patience. He does not require of you more than He is prepared to give you. He will do for you exceeding abundantly above what you ask or even think![5]

SERVING BRINGS JOY

True joy flows from knowing God and worshiping Him for who He is—the breathing out of the love and strength that God has breathed into us. That service is a path to joy.

Unhappiness is so often tied to an inward focus, where we give our needs, our wants, our hurts, our complaints way too much attention. God cares about every detail of our lives. But that doesn't mean He wants us to live there, serving ourselves.

Serving forces us to take our eyes off our needs and put them on the needs of others. It opens the pipeline of God's love, where we both receive and give. Proverbs 11:25 says this: "A generous person will prosper; whoever refreshes others will be refreshed" (NIV).

James Russell Miller, a popular preacher from the early 1900s, puts it this way:

> There is one kind of living, however, which more than any other, contains the master secret of joy. It is a life of service. It begins in consecration to Christ: we must, first of all, be His servants. It includes trust—reposing upon God. But there can be no continued quiet confidence, if there be no activity in Christian life. Still water stagnates. Even trust without action, soon loses its restfulness.
>
> Work itself is always a helper of happiness. Indolence is never truly happy. The happiest man—is the busy man. Even physical health depends largely upon regular occupation. No man, able for duty, who is not busy, can be truly or deeply happy. The idle man may be living a life of pleasure—but it is not a life of real happiness. Work is a condition of joy.[6]

When we serve, we stay fresh. When we serve, we fulfill the two greatest commands of loving God and loving our neighbor. When we serve, we minister directly to Jesus. When we serve, we open the flow of grace and strength into our lives. When we serve, we experience an abiding joy. Proverbs 11:25 says, "A generous person will prosper; whoever refreshes others will be refreshed" (NIV).

What will you do for Jesus today in love and worship? How will you serve Him to glorify His name? Look around you and ask Jesus to show you needs that you can meet today. Rejoice and thank God that yours is a life of purpose! Because Jesus came and lived, died, and rose again for *people*, when we serve others and lay down our lives for those in need, it is then we are most Christlike. . . . *Selah*.

MY MISSION

For I have come down from heaven
to do the will of God who sent me,
not to do my own will.

JOHN 6:38

I'LL NEVER FORGET SITTING in South African dirt with a beautiful four-year-old boy in an orphanage in Johannesburg. It seemed nothing could reach his lonely little heart—not toys or games or treats. Not even the crazy young musicians traveling with us, who lavished attention and smiles on him, could find a way to connect. His eyes were glazed over. He would not speak or respond to our efforts.

Is it possible to give up on life and hope and others at age four? I cannot bear to think about what he had already endured at such a young age.

So there in the dirt I simply sat down and started singing "Jesus Loves Me." It only took moments for his beautiful, tear-filled eyes to look up, and all I can say is that our hearts connected. I sang, and we stared deep into each other's heart. He lifted his hand and touched my cheek with his finger. We built Jesus a throne in the middle of the dirt and worshiped together.

No matter what churches and temples and cathedrals you've visited, I promise you, none was as grand as the sanctuary I

90

worshiped in that morning. Built by the Father himself, it was a place of spirit and truth.

As we drew near to God, He drew near to us. That's the promise of worshiping God. There is no other name like the name of Jesus to heal our wounds, calm our fears, walk with us through suffering, and to even hold an aching four-year-old tenderly in His arms. The boy's heart was opened to the love of Jesus, and he experienced what a Samaritan woman did centuries earlier. He drew from a well that could never be taken from him and would never run dry.

In twelve months of cancer treatments, I may not have been able to lead worship through music, but the mission of my life *as a worshiper* did not change one bit. As I sat in doctors' waiting rooms and lay in hospital beds during treatments and recovery, the call to take Jesus to every sacred place I set my foot still burned in me just like leading people to His glorious courts through praise does.

WORSHIP AND MISSION

As I've prayed about this book, about all that worship means, my heart always connects worship to mission. These two words are like fire in my belly; they daily give me my purpose and reason for living. They are not the same thing, but it is a thin veil that separates them from one another. Worship and mission are almost like a bride and groom—it is hard to have a wedding with just one of them.

Mission will always be trumped by worship, for worship abides forever. But as we continue to create His throne room here among us, building His glorious throne of praise and going deeper in our understanding and experience of worship, we discover mission. We witness with our hearts and feel deep in our spirit the *passion* God has for the lost and broken. In worship we feel God's heart—His mission—that *everyone* needs to hear, see, and know the goodness of the gospel.

Jesus is the Author and Perfecter of our faith. We are to keep our eyes fixed on Him as we run the marathon of life. Consider why He came in God's Word, and you will see so vividly the connection between worship and mission.

- He came to shine light in darkness: "I have come as a light to shine in this dark world, so that all who put their trust in me will no longer remain in the dark" (John 12:46).

- He came to preach and deliver: "Jesus said, 'Let's go to the rest of the villages so I can preach there also. This is why I've come.'" He went to their meeting places all through Galilee, preaching and throwing out the demons" (Mark 1:38-39 THE MESSAGE).

- He came to do His Father's will: "For I have come down from heaven to do the will of God who sent me, not to do my own will" (John 6:38).

- He came to seek the lost: "Jesus said, 'Today is salvation day in this home! Here he is: Zacchaeus, son of Abraham! For the Son of Man came to find and restore the lost'" (Luke 19:10 THE MESSAGE).

- He came to save sinners: "Here's a word you can take to heart and depend on: Jesus Christ came into the world to save sinners. I'm proof—Public Sinner Number One—of someone who could never have made it apart from sheer mercy" (1 Timothy 1:15 THE MESSAGE).

- He came to serve: "For even the Son of Man came not to be served but to serve others and to give his life as a ransom for many" (Matthew 20:28).

- He came to pay the ultimate price, to suffer and die for our sins with a willing heart and praise for the Father on His lips: "Right now I am storm-tossed. And what am I going to say? 'Father, get me out of this'? No, this is why I came in the first place. I'll say, 'Father, put your glory on display'" (John 12:27-28 THE MESSAGE).

- He came to show the full extent of God's love for us: "In this is love: not that we loved God, but that He loved us and sent His Son to be the propitiation (the atoning sacrifice) for our sins" (1 John 4:10 AMPLIFIED).

Did you notice just how interwoven mission and worship were for Jesus? As He does the Father's will and fulfills His mission to us, He brings glory to the Father's name.

If you are missing a sense of purpose and mission in life, begin with worship. Praise the Father with everything you have and are. I guarantee your specific calling, your specific mission—of serving, loving, ministering, witnessing, blessing, giving—will emerge. Don't stop until you find it!

For how can truthful worship be anything but missional? In genuine worship we are constantly declaring God's goodness, always announcing that He is with us, always being filled with joy in His presence, always announcing freedom, always dependent on the Holy Spirit to fill us, change us, lead us, and turn our sorrows into joy and our mourning into dancing.

To worship with our life means that it is not just in the singing of songs that we find our hearts emblazoned with His presence and passion; it spills over into life where His passion—our mission—finds its expression in the going, the sending, and the daily expression of our faith in the ordinary. As Christ followers, all that we are should somehow result in bringing the love and light of Christ to our world. Is this mission? Oh yes. Is this worship? Absolutely!

PEOPLE NEED THE LORD. . . . PEOPLE NEED YOU

Throughout the writing of this book, I have found my heart drawn back to John 4 over and over. It is the account of when Jesus discusses truthful worship with the Samaritan woman. It is the account of Jesus seeing a person everyone else ignored and offering her a living water that changed her life forever. It worked in and through her so deeply that this outcast became a witness of Jesus' love to her entire town.

But it is also an account where Jesus puts a challenge to His followers, then and now:

> "The food that keeps me going is that I do the will of the One who sent me, finishing the work he started. As you look around right now, wouldn't you say that in about four months it will be time to harvest? Well, I'm telling you to open your eyes and take a good look at what's right in front of you. These Samaritan fields are ripe. It's harvest time!"

> John 4:34-35 THE MESSAGE

As we fix our eyes on Jesus worship, it is time we open our eyes to the needs all around us. People are lost and so damaged. In worship God will remind us that people throughout history and today have tried and try desperately to fill a void in their soul—maybe with alcohol, drugs, food, activity, sex, or nonstop media entertainment—but all of it is futile. No matter what we use to fill the void, if it isn't God, it will leave the same hole in our soul filled with anger, confusion, regret, and alienation. For there is a place in the heart of mankind that is reserved for Christ Jesus himself, and nothing else will satisfy the longing.

What we have to offer is the same thing Peter offered—Jesus. Then Peter said, "Silver or gold I do not have, but what I do have I give you. In the name of Jesus Christ of Nazareth, walk" (Acts 3:16 NIV).

We bring Jesus to the world in our witness and compassion. Having His presence within us, we take Him wherever we go.

Wherever I travel, wherever Jesus is being preached, my heart is filled with joy as I hear the bold challenge for Christ's followers to be bearers of justice and grace, to literally stand in the great divide between abundance and abject poverty, and serve as a bridge of sacrifice and love. My heart is stirred by the trumpet call to be the hands and feet of Jesus to the hurting and dying of the world.

There have been parts of the church that have been beautiful bearers of love, justice, and compassion for years. One of the most powerful statements of saving the lost is found in the vision of William Booth, founder of the Salvation Army.

I saw a dark and stormy ocean. Over it the black clouds hung heavily; through them every now and then vivid lightening flashed and loud thunder rolled, while the winds moaned, and the waves rose and foamed, towered and broke, only to rise and foam, tower and break again.

In that ocean I thought I saw myriads of poor human beings plunging and floating, shouting and shrieking, cursing and struggling and drowning; and as they cursed and screamed they rose and shrieked again, and then some sank to rise no more.

And I saw out of this dark angry ocean, a mighty rock that rose up with its summit towering high above the black clouds that overhung the stormy sea. And all around the base of this great rock I saw a vast platform. Onto this platform, I saw with delight a number of the poor struggling, drowning wretches continually climbing out of the angry ocean. And I saw that a few of those who were already safe on the platform were helping the poor creatures still in the angry waters to reach the place of safety. . . .

Does the surging sea look dark and dangerous? Unquestionably it is so. There is no doubt that the leap for you, as for everyone who takes it, means difficulty and scorn and suffering. For you it may mean more than this. It may mean death. He who beckons you from the sea however, knows what it will mean—and knowing, He still calls to you and bids to you to come.

You must do it! You cannot hold back. You have enjoyed yourself in Christianity long enough. You have had pleasant feelings, pleasant songs, pleasant meetings, pleasant prospects. There has been much of human happiness, much clapping of hands and shouting of praises—very much of heaven on earth.

Now then, go to God and tell Him you are prepared as much as necessary to turn your back upon it all, and that you are willing to spend the rest of your days struggling in the midst of these perishing multitudes, whatever it may cost you.

You must do it. With the light that is now broken in upon your mind and the call that is now sounding in your ears, and the beckoning hands that are now before your eyes, you have no alternative. To go down among the perishing crowds is your duty. Your happiness from now on will consist in sharing their misery, your ease in sharing their pain, your crown in helping them to bear their cross, and your heaven in going into the very jaws of hell to rescue them.[1]

Booth concluded his booklet by asking: "Now what will you do?" What will you and I do?

Oh my. Aren't you ready to put this book down and go rescue someone? Serve someone? Love someone?

Justice, mercy, compassion, and love for all people have been beautifully proclaimed through the centuries of the church—but sadly, it is sometimes ignored.

But as I travel, I am witnessing a mighty wake-up call deep in the spirits of followers and churches and missions all over the world. It defies geography and theological and denominational differences. It often comes from the young, but I've seen believers of all ages rise to answer the groan of humanity.

I believe it is part of a revival of worship. It sounds like the song of praise in Isaiah 61:10-11:

I am overwhelmed with joy in the Lord my God! For he has dressed me with the clothing of salvation and draped me in a robe of righteousness. I am like a bridegroom dressed for his wedding or a bride with her jewels. The Sovereign Lord will show his justice to the nations of the world. Everyone will praise him! His righteousness will be like a garden in early spring, with plants springing up everywhere.

Your mission will begin in worship of God but find its expression as the Holy Spirit opens your eyes to the needs of humanity and asks you to respond with compassion.

Jesus came, lived, and died for His Father and for all people. *Not my will but thine.* He came to lift the lives of people, always stopping when His heart was moved with compassion, taking time for those who lived in the shadows of shame or were castaways, the ones no one even noticed.

As we continue to reveal Jesus in worship and in every area of our lives, I see God's throne being established among us in our churches, in our communities, in our families, in our new experiences, and in our traditions. Wherever He is enthroned, you will find true worshipers with eyes wide open to the needs of the lost and needy.

That's worship. That's mission.

KEEP IT SIMPLE—JUST STOP AND MEET A NEED

Worship is a place of joy. But the ultimate purpose of worship is not only that we leave our meetings feeling good about ourselves and God's life in us; it is that in His presence we hear Him speak, we feel what He feels, we are changed, and we declare His power and presence in the midst of our world in both words and actions.

Darlene, this sounds like too much. I'm no William Booth—I can't recruit and organize something like the Salvation Army. I care deeply about people, but I'm not a Mother Teresa; I can't move to Calcutta—I have a family to raise. I want to see people saved, but I can't preach like Billy Graham. I like music, but I can't write hymns like Charles Wesley or do like his brother John and ride horseback to preach to millions. I'm just me. Ordinary me.

We have shown how worship leads us to bring justice and mercy to the world, but where do we start?

It starts with ordinary people like you and me getting captured by the love and power of our extraordinary God. We worship and we open our eyes to the world around us. We listen to the

Spirit, who speaks in a calm, peace-filled, small voice whispering, "You could do something here. You could make a difference. You could change a situation for someone." Worship. Watch. Listen. Ask.

Ask God to give you ears to hear and eyes to see like He does. In all honesty, I don't know that we could ever fully hear and see as God does, for the anguish would break us. But we can resist the temptation to shut out the troubles of the world and naïvely hope someone else will do what we are ignoring and neglecting.

A friend of mine illustrates this simplicity beautifully. She was going through a personal revival and was attuned to God and His Spirit. She asked Him to give her an opportunity to get involved in helping others more than she had in the past. God answered her prayer almost immediately—He is listening! The very next day as she was driving, she looked out her side window and saw a girl wandering along the road by herself. She was stumbling and seemed very disoriented. Cars continued to zoom by, putting the girl in a precarious situation.

My friend noticed someone in need who was seemingly invisible to everyone else. That was first—just like Jesus with the Samaritan woman. Then she stopped. That doesn't sound very hard, but no one else was doing it. She circled back, rolled down her car window, and asked if help was needed. The girl couldn't seem to understand the question, so she couldn't provide an answer. My friend got involved. She got the girl in the car, and with difficulty and patience was able to find her home.

That would be enough for most of us, but God really was at work in her heart. She asked what more she could do to help. Did the girl need money or food? Did she have someone to talk to?

There's more I could tell, but the story isn't finished, praise God.

My friend did nothing remarkable. She prayed, she noticed, she stopped, she helped. But in so doing she gave the young girl the gifts of dignity and the feeling of love just by speaking to her. She offered her living water and a chance to have a new start.

Don't make mission complicated. Love God. Love people. Be who you are. Don't do it for credit or so that you are noticed. There's a lot of things I can't do. But I can sing "Jesus Loves Me" to a little boy in the dirt in South Africa.

What is your mission? What has God called you to do?

You will find that the situations that stir you to bring change are directly connected to your life's purpose. Use what is in your hand today to outwork what is in your heart.

CHAPTER 9

MY LOVE FOR OTHERS

Love bears up under anything and everything that comes,
is ever ready to believe the best of every person, its hopes are fadeless
under all circumstances, and it endures everything
[without weakening]. Love never fails [never fades out
or becomes obsolete or comes to an end].

1 CORINTHIANS 13:7-8 AMPLIFIED

LOVE IS A WORD that is used so much it has been trivialized and watered down. It is used *all* the time—sometimes well, but sometimes very poorly. We listen to songs about love that move us, and see movies about love that may cause our hearts to sing. Meanwhile, we say we love a movie, we love pizza, or we love a flower. And then we hear the phrase from the Word: "Love never fails." Yet we know that the kind of love humanity offers fails all the time. But the Word of God offers a whole new definition of love that goes far beyond what we like and enjoy.

Agape is the word that describes God's love. It is a love that is so big and so wide and so deep. There is no finer, higher, or more excellent kind of love—it is inexhaustible and indescribable. It is a love that puts the highest value on human life and honors each other's needs. It is a love that can only come from God and find its full expression in the worship of God. For when we honor God it becomes as natural as breathing that we honor others. Agape is a love that is so huge that the one receiving it has no choice but to respond.

In the Greek of the New Testament, *eros* love defines sexual intimacy and is beautiful in a committed relationship that is already filled with agape love. It cannot replace agape love because it can be expressed only to fulfill your own needs. It breaks my heart that so many are so hungry and desperate to be loved that they have settled for eros love as an end in and of itself.

The Greek also refers to *stergo* love, which describes our feelings within a family setting. As wonderful as it is to feel the bonds of family love, it does not go as deep as the self-giving nature of agape love.

Then there is *phileo* love, where people fulfill each other's needs in the bonds of friendship. We know how comforting that is. It gives us a very needed sense of connection. It is a gift from God. It builds churches, families, and communities. But it still doesn't reach to the depths of agape love.

Agape love is when we honor the other person with no strings attached. Even if there's nothing in it for me. Even if it's not a family member. Even if I don't feel the connection of liking someone. Agape love is me pouring out what God has poured into my heart through His love that reached out to me even when I was unlovable and didn't love Him back. It is a spiritual act of obedience and worship. There will never be enough wonderful words to describe this love!

Agape is a purely giving love—so deep and so huge that you don't even care about what the response will be. You decide to love the one to whom the love is directed without thought of self. It is the highest level of loving someone.

It is no wonder the word *agape* is so difficult to translate. In fact, scholars have been baffled for centuries over this one word, for it is a word so filled with emotion and depth that we could try to offer descriptions of it all day and yet still never come close to the breadth of its meaning. It is indescribable.

There is only one love like this, because it is a supernatural expression of what God has done inside us. This love is born of the Holy Spirit at work. Galatians 5:22 says, "But the Holy Spirit produces this kind of fruit in our lives: love, joy, peace, patience, kindness, goodness, faithfulness." Paul is telling us that the first fruit of the Spirit is love—agape love. We can't generate it—any more than a telephone pole could suddenly start bearing apples or pears or bananas. This agape love is born of worship. It is the breath of God inside us—the same breath that gave Adam and Eve life. When we exhale, only then can we give the gift of agape. It is the most excellent way, the most beautiful expression we have of Christ in us. The hope of glory, the hope of Christ seen within us. To flow in this kind of love out of striving or out of self-motivation is just impossible. We often think we are going to try to *do our best* and love that person *one more time*. The problem with this is that when we fail, we fall under condemnation.

If you are feeling almost detached from this agape love that I'm speaking of, let me remind you that the potential for this love is already within you—sown as the seed of the promise of God's Word in your own spirit. As you focus on Jesus' love for you, this most perfect love will simply begin to flow out from you.

FEAR IS REPLACED
BY POWERFUL WITNESS

When I was growing up in church, I often heard that the opposite of fear is faith—just have more faith, and then you will not be afraid. I would try and try to muster up more faith, and every time I failed, I just got more down on myself. But I have discovered over time that the antidote to all our fears is agape love: "There is no fear in love. But perfect love drives out fear, because fear has to do with punishment. The one who fears is not made perfect in love" (1 John 4:18 NIV).

But how can love cast out fear? That sounds too good to be true! Not with God. Joyce Meyer shares so poignantly *and practically* about her own powerful fears and how love cast fear from her life:

Because I had been abused in my childhood and was fearful of being hurt or taken advantage of, I became very insecure. And I spent many years trying to control everything and everyone in my life. Instead of trying to control and manipulate people, I needed to learn to trust God, pray, and believe that He would do what was best for me at the right time. Most of all, I needed to abide in His love.[1]

God's *agape* love meets the deepest needs of our lives. We experience it in worship and it changes everything—even to the point of casting out fear! Fear is replaced by a boldness in sharing the miracle of God's love for us to the entire world:

> "So now I am giving you a new commandment: Love each other. Just as I have loved you, you should love each other. Your love for one another will prove to the world that you are my disciples."
>
> John 13:34-35

The love described here is agape love—the far-reaching, ever-forgiving love that will be the thing that announces to the world that we are His disciples. The love that gives without asking for anything in return.

The world does not comprehend agape love. This is where the global church is set apart from those outside of Christ—in our service to the broken. The love that is driving our agendas is a love born of the Spirit. It doesn't "run out" when we are weary. God's love just keeps filling our hearts.

Mother Teresa said, "I have found the paradox, that if you love until it hurts, there can be no more hurt, only more love."[2] That is a love that transcends fear and changes the world!

TRANSFORMED RELATIONSHIPS

Agape love is so simple, but it still takes a lifetime to let seep into the depths of our souls. It comes as we worship God in His holiness, as we proclaim His goodness and majesty. For that's where agape is modeled for us and poured into our lives. God does not *demand* that we love Him back. He loves us because He loves us. Period. Bottom line. He doesn't love us because we respond to Him—His love patiently waits for us.

Imagine what could happen if this kind of love existed between a husband and a wife. Even when we are angry, even when we feel we are not being heard, even when we struggle with our temper, even when we feel completely disappointed—our response is to ask the Lord to allow His agape love to flow out of our lives. What a difference that would make in our marriages.

If agape love is the basis of our family relationships, rather than just stergo love, we will experience so much more grace to stand together in tough times, rather than just out of obligation. If agape love is the basis of the intimate relationship between husband and wife, then each one will seek to serve and please their spouse rather than be self-focused. It will change our relationships with parents, children, and siblings! If agape love is the basis of our dear friendships, rather than just phileo, then our friendships will remain strong and steadfast, not needy and insecure, whether or not we benefit from the relationship. Healthy friendships are not controlling, manipulative, emotionally fragile, or continually charged and volatile. We need agape love to sustain healthy, life-giving friendships.

If agape love is the basis of our lives, we will totally change as the difference in us is worked out in our day-to-day interactions with the ones we are called to do life with. This is the unconditional love we all crave and desire.

This is not our natural inclination. That's why in 1 Corinthians 14:1, Paul urges us to follow after charity: "Follow the way of love and eagerly desire gifts of the Spirit" (NIV).

The word for "follow" here in the Greek is *doioko*, which means to hotly, passionately pursue something. It is an act of diligence. As we honor others, it becomes our chief pursuit and aim to express what God has done inside of us!

Start there. Have you fully experienced and embraced God's love for you? We've spoken of His love throughout this book. But has it sunk deep down in your spirit? When it does—watch out! You will love others as never before! But it begins with receiving God's love in your own life first. Brennan Manning said, "I could more easily contain Niagara Falls in a tea cup than I can comprehend the wild, uncontainable love of God."[3] It overflows, splashing and then soaking our relationships!

When God looked upon the human race as we were lost in our sin, we were so precious to Him that He had to do something. This agape love drove Him to action. This love knows no limits. He sacrificed His beloved Son on our behalf. He did this for the sake of you and me, the people He so deeply cherished. And we share this love with the world:

> Dear friends, let us continue to love one another, for love comes from God. Anyone who loves is a child of God and knows God. But anyone who does not love does not know God, for God is love.
>
> God showed how much he loved us by sending his one and only Son into the world so that we might have eternal life through him. This is real love—not that we loved God, but that he loved us and sent his Son as a sacrifice to take away our sins.
>
> 1 John 4:7-10

It doesn't matter what you've done, where you find yourself today, how big the rejections have been in your life. This is the love you have been looking for and the love you are called to give!

Are you sharing with others what God shared with you as you magnify Him? Are you willing to give your very life for those you love? "There is no greater love than to lay down one's life for one's friends" (John 15:13).

FORGIVENESS—THE PERFECTION OF LOVE

We experience the lavish love that God has for us in the atonement, in the sacrifice He made to bring us back in relationship with Him: "But God demonstrates his own love for us in this: While we were still sinners, Christ died for us" (Romans 5:8 NIV).

Not long ago I popped down to the town of Terrigal to buy some food when suddenly a young guy on a skateboard came flying around the corner and knocked down an older woman who was crossing the road. She fell with a huge thump. I ran over, as did others, to help out. She was suffering from neck damage and it was very scary for her.

While we were waiting for the ambulance, the lady's husband arrived. They both became very emotional—they were very connected—and were visibly shaken and in shock. But the young man stood off to the side. He didn't run off; he waited and was in shock himself. The police made him wait it out. This young man was so mad at himself and was becoming more and more anxious by the moment. I stood with him and assured him that all would be well.

After the ambulance left, the husband walked over and offered his hand to the young man and said, "Son, it was an accident." He offered his hand in forgiveness. You could see a burden of guilt and worry fall from the young man's shoulders. I believe it was a life-changing moment for him. As I started walking back to my car, I felt like I had witnessed a firsthand experience of the grace and power of forgiveness in action yet again. As broken humanity came in contact with forgiveness, grace won. The story could have played out very differently depending on the husband's response.

Perhaps this small encounter cannot come close to describing the hurt that has been done to you. But forgiveness is still the most profound human expression of God's agape love you can show.

In the Sermon on the Mount, Jesus teaches the people—and us:

"You have heard the law that says, 'Love your neighbor' and hate your enemy. But I say, love your enemies! Pray for those who persecute you! In that way, you will be acting as true children of your Father in heaven. For he gives his sunlight to both the evil and the good, and he sends rain on the just and the unjust alike. If you love only those who love you, what reward is there for that? Even corrupt tax collectors do that much. If you are kind only to your friends, how are you different from anyone else? Even pagans do that. But you are to be perfect, even as your Father in heaven is perfect."

Matthew 5:43-48

As we've talked about agape love, perhaps you've nodded your head in agreement: *I want to love my spouse like that. I want to show love to my brothers and sisters in Christ like that. I want to show and teach that kind of love to my children. I want to share such love with my friends.* But now we are talking about forgiving and loving the most difficult people in life—those who have deliberately hurt us: our enemies, evildoers, people we don't like!

Notice that Jesus said we are to be perfect as our heavenly Father is perfect. This is exactly what He is referring to: loving the world—everyone in the world—like He does! Perfection is when God's love for us spills onto those who don't love us.

Forgiveness is worship—you've received it and now you share it. It has the absolute power to bring freedom in your life. When we practice forgiveness, the flow of love casts out not only fear but the hatred and resentments that would rob us of our spiritual vitality—and rob us of freely worshiping God. Jesus continues His sermon to the disciples by teaching them to pray. And His model prayer tells us that we come to God by saying, "Forgive us our sins, as we have forgiven those who sin against us" (Matthew 6:12).

By contrast, when we harbor unforgiveness, it limits our heart capacity to receive and share agape love. It will accompany us on the road to poor choices, and in many cases will cause our physical bodies to become sick. It is amazing how much all of us have the tendency to hold on to unforgiveness.

The Word of God is weighty with Scriptures on the importance of forgiveness:

> Get rid of all bitterness, rage, anger, harsh words, and slander, as well as all types of evil behavior. Instead, be kind to each other, tenderhearted, forgiving one another, just as God through Christ has forgiven you.
>
> Ephesians 4:31-32

Forgiveness is the ultimate test of agape. I know in my own life how many times a day I need to apply forgiveness. As any sense of grievance or grudge or condemning spirit comes into my mind, I need to apply forgiveness—to others, to myself—proclaiming freedom! Living free from bitterness, disappointment, and resentment is a real trick, but this is our inheritance as Christians. Listen to the whisper—or shout—of the Holy Spirit to forgive and to set free.

WITHHOLDING LOVE AND FORGIVENESS IS A NEW SLAVERY

In Matthew 18 Jesus shares a story that we call the parable of the unmerciful servant:

> "Therefore, the Kingdom of heaven can be compared to a king who decided to bring his accounts up to date with servants who had borrowed money from him. In the process, one of his debtors was brought in who owed him millions of dollars. He couldn't pay, so his master ordered that he be sold—along with his wife, his children, and everything he owned—to pay the debt.
>
> "But the man fell down before his master and begged him, 'Please, be patient with me, and I will pay it all.' Then his master was filled with pity for him, and he released him and forgave his debt.

"But when the man left the king, he went to a fellow servant who owed him a few thousand dollars. He grabbed him by the throat and demanded instant payment.

"His fellow servant fell down before him and begged for a little more time. 'Be patient with me, and I will pay it,' he pleaded. But his creditor wouldn't wait. He had the man arrested and put in prison until the debt could be paid in full.

"When some of the other servants saw this, they were very upset. They went to the king and told him everything that had happened. Then the king called in the man he had forgiven and said, 'You evil servant! I forgave you that tremendous debt because you pleaded with me. Shouldn't you have mercy on your fellow servant, just as I had mercy on you?' Then the angry king sent the man to prison to be tortured until he had paid his entire debt.

"That's what my heavenly Father will do to you if you refuse to forgive your brothers and sisters from your heart."

Matthew 18:23-35

Forgiveness . . . the ultimate expression of agape love . . . is at the crux of everything God is about and everything the Bible says. Are you struggling with forgiveness? Let God speak to your heart. Ponder what He has done for you. Listen as He says to you, "When My Son died on the cross, that was my way of showing you the full extent of how much I love you. That is my most precious gift to you. That is my doorway to eternity for you. I now ask you to open that door to everyone in your life, even those who have harmed you. Be united with me in love."

My friend, are you harboring anger and bitterness because of the sins others have committed against you? It will bind you in slavery to your past! T.D. Jakes said, "We cannot embrace God's forgiveness if we are so busy clinging to past wounds and nursing old grudges."[4]

Unforgiveness will lead to internal emotional turmoil. It means that we are permanently tied to the act of sin against us.

We cannot get over it or get release from it and move on with our lives until we forgive the person and put the consequences of their actions into God's hands to deal with. Bad things that have been done to us in the past cannot be changed. But having grudges does not help us, nor does it hurt the person we hold the grudge against. The other party has sinned against us and moved on with their life, but we cannot detach ourselves and move on until we give it over to God and forgive them.

Forgiveness allows our hearts to start healing. It is often a slow process if the emotions have been bottled up for many years. We need to remember that forgiving someone is showing them mercy that they do not deserve—just as God through sending His Son to die for our sins gave us mercy that we did not deserve. The amazing thing is that when we forgive someone else, God's love blooms and blossoms within us. Isn't it just like God to take that which someone else meant to harm us to make us stronger, more alive, and yes, even more joyful in His presence? It's a miracle of grace.

If you still don't *feel* like forgiving, let me remind you, forgiveness is not an emotion, it is a personal choice. We have to choose to forgive and keep on choosing it. When we do this, we cut the ties to the emotional hurts and can begin to heal. Forgiveness releases us from the bondage of resentment and bitterness and gives us freedom and peace.

I pray that you will find the freedom of forgiveness that Joseph experienced, which enabled him to be reconciled to his brothers and to minister to them for his own good, the good of his family, the good of his people, and most of all to the glory of God. Are you still reluctant to experience forgiveness in your own life? I pray that you will find the freedom of forgiveness that Saul accepted with gratitude, turning him from a murderer to an ambassador of reconciliation.

Worship changes everything, for it opens our hearts and lives to the flow of God's kindness, mercy, grace, forgiveness, and agape with everyone we encounter!

MY ATTITUDE

Shout with joy to the Lord, all the earth!
Worship the Lord with gladness.
Come before him, singing with joy.

PSALM 100:1-2

EMOTIONS ARE SPONTANEOUS FEELINGS in response to something outside of us. We see a car swerve into our lane of traffic and we feel fear. We get a call and learn that a good friend we grew up with has died and we feel sorrow. We receive news our daughter is going to have a baby—and we are going to become grandparents—and oh, we feel joy. So much joy.

Flash emotions are not something we consciously control in the split second they explode. Attitudes, on the other hand, though expressed in emotions, combine how we feel, think, and behave about something.

In his classic motivational book *The Life Triumphant*, James Allen, drawing from the wisdom of the Proverbs, teaches,

> A man has to learn that he cannot command things, but that he can command himself; that he cannot coerce the wills of others, but that he can mold and master his own will: and things serve him who serves Truth; people seek guidance of him who is master of himself.[1]

111

In another classic work of his, *As a Man Thinketh*, Allen adds,

> The man who sows wrong thoughts and deeds and prays that God will bless him is in the position of a farmer who, having sown tares, asks God to bring forth for him a harvest of wheat.[2]

As a man thinketh—as you think, as I think, *in Christ*—that will determine our attitudes and have a huge positive or negative impact on our emotions. Am I aligning my thoughts with Jesus' thoughts?

Too many brothers and sisters in Christ have come to salvation but remain captive in a prison of emotions that have soured and become toxic. Unfettered negativity, a critical spirit, anger, jealousy, depression (the list goes on) will rob you and everyone else around you of joy.

Please don't misread me. Emotions are real and will spring up outside our volition. There are periods of life when there is so much upheaval and pain all around us that it is only natural to get flooded with negative emotions. And if you are one who walks through life carrying deep depression, then my love and prayers are with you. I had never experienced real anxiety until last year when walking through chemotherapy. I would feel it begin in my toes and travel through my body until it got to my heart, and I felt like I could die unless someone rescued me. But firsthand, I am thrilled to offer the good news and hope that as we truly release God's worship and His promise over our lives, our homes, and our hearts, He is magnified above the pain, and kingdom reign is reestablished again in our lives. This is the beauty of worship. When we come as we are, exalting Jesus Christ above all, experiencing His power and presence, His grace *again* is experienced fresh in that very moment. It begins when we offer our bodies as living sacrifices—we give ourselves completely to God, which is our spiritual worship, which leads to a renewed mind that is not conformed to the patterns of this world but is an outflowing of

God's thoughts, God's will, God's love, and God's spirit inside and outside of us.

The good news and hope I offer means you do not need to be a victim of circumstances; you are a victor in Christ Jesus!

The source of that hope is God's love. Your means for securing that love is through simply yielding to the great love of God, allowing Him to shape and mold you and all you think about and respond to. Our attitudes are transformed as we decide to let go and let the Holy Spirit do His work in us. This means replacing negative thoughts and mindsets, arresting our attitudes that we know will not be of benefit.

I pray we won't miss just how important our attitudes are—how they affect our worship and how they are transformed by worship. Much loved and respected Bible teacher Charles Swindoll puts the immediate and eternal importance of our attitudes this way:

> The longer I live, the more I realize the impact of attitude on life. Attitude, to me, is more important than facts. It is more important than the past, than education, than money, than circumstances, than failures, than successes, than what other people think or say or do. It is more important than appearance, giftedness or skill. It will make or break a company . . . a church . . . a home. The remarkable thing is we have a choice every day regarding the attitude we will embrace for that day. We cannot change our past. . . . We cannot change the fact that people will act in a certain way. We cannot change the inevitable. The only thing we can do is play on the one string we have, and that is our attitude. . . . I am convinced that life is 10% what happens to me and 90% how I react to it. And so it is with you . . . we are in charge of our attitudes.[3]

CHOOSE JOY, CHOOSE FREEDOM

Some would say we have no choice in our attitudes—that how we feel, think, and act are determined by genetics or circumstances.

They make the joyful attitude nothing more than a flash of happiness. A warm, positive response to circumstances of life. But the biblical writers knew joy was something much deeper than a response to circumstances. They saw it as an attitude that comes as a gift from God when we choose to see blessings and favor, no matter what is going on around us. Joy is a fruit of the Spirit, is not reserved for the "sanguine types," and is available to us all.

That's why our Lord's brother James could begin his letter to scattered, persecuted, beleaguered Christians: "Dear brothers and sisters, when troubles of any kind come your way, consider it an opportunity for great joy" (James 1:2). Joy is something to be considered in the mind, an activity of our will and thoughts. It is something to be chosen. Or as Jesus taught in the Sermon on the Mount,

> "What blessings await you when people hate you and exclude you and mock you and curse you as evil because you follow the Son of Man. When that happens, be happy! Yes, leap for joy! For a great reward awaits you in heaven. And remember, their ancestors treated the ancient prophets that same way."
>
> Luke 6:22–23

Jesus didn't say to people that they would automatically feel happy and blessed. The verb tense for the simple word *be* is active, not passive. Did you catch that? It is something we choose and do!

Proverbs 16:32 tells us, "He who is slow to anger is better than the mighty, and he who rules his spirit, than he who captures a city" (NASB). A person who knows how to manage their emotions is more powerful than a warrior who captures a fortified city. Negative emotions left to grow like a weed taking root can be such a destructive force in one's life. It's like pulling all the oxygen from a room. No air, no room to move. We all know someone who is held captive by negative thoughts and feelings. All it takes is a little push on the trigger of that emotion to set it off. One reminder of a painful, difficult moment from the past and they immediately hurdle down a self-defeating spiral.

No wonder we need to worship. No wonder worship changes everything. For it is in the decision—the exercise of our will—to worship that our whole perspective on life changes. Our eyes are drawn to God, our Protector and Healer. We no longer obsess over what is wrong with life, but we learn to simply breathe and find joy in the opportunities to grow, to conquer, to bless, to draw nearer to our Lord and Savior.

If your emotions are defeating you right now, I would encourage you to look deeply and see if your attitudes are fueling negative emotions or fighting and transforming them into something beautiful.

Don Colbert, M.D., in his book *Deadly Emotions*, writes:

> I've worked with countless people who have discovered that once they made a sincere effort to tackle their dysfunctional thought patterns, they had fewer bouts of depression, anxiety, anger, fear, shame, jealousy, and all other toxic emotions. It isn't difficult to replace lies with God's truth. It just takes intentional and consistent effort. . . . It takes the time and energy to find statements of God's truth and apply them to life's lies.[4]

Colbert points to the Scripture that shows how to tackle Satan's lies and the thought patterns that tear down our emotions rather than build them up:

> So Jesus said to those Jews who had believed in Him, If you abide in My word [hold fast to My teachings and live in accordance with them], you are truly My disciples. And you will know the Truth, and the Truth will set you free.
>
> John 8:31-32 Amplified

Are you abiding in God's Word? Are you believing what His Word says about who you are, or are you believing the lies of the world? Are you seeing the world with the eyes of the flesh or the Spirit?

We discover and express joy through worship by where we set our eyes and hearts. David chose the joy found in worship when he said, "How lovely is your dwelling place, O Lord of Heaven's Armies. I long, yes, I faint with longing to enter the courts of the Lord. With my whole being, body and soul, I will shout joyfully to the living God" (Psalm 84:1-2). Paul puts it so powerfully when he reminds us,

> Since you have been raised to new life with Christ, set your sights on the realities of heaven, where Christ sits in the place of honor at God's right hand. Think about the things of heaven, not the things of earth. For you died to this life, and your real life is hidden with Christ in God. And when Christ, who is your life, is revealed to the whole world, you will share in all his glory.
>
> Colossians 3:1-4

Because of God's love for us, we have been raised from the dead, from the spiritual death of sin, and are allowed to see this world from the perspective of eternity. We can know in our hearts that we will appear with Him in glory.

What happens when we look to heaven and see our Lord and Savior? Paul tells us we are given the fuel and power to turn from earthly contaminants: immorality, impurity, lust, evil desires, and greed (see Colossians 3:5). We are likewise empowered to rid our hearts and thoughts of the emotions that would curse our lives: anger, rage, malice, slander, and filthy language (v. 8).

Instead, our new vision of the world puts us in a place where we can put on a new self, renewed in the knowledge and image of our Creator (v. 10). And what a different self that is! We are compassionate, kind, humble, gentle, and patient, and we can bear with each other's faults and forgive. We are bound together in love and unity (vv. 12-14).

All that is wonderful, but Paul goes on to say that when we set our eyes above, on heavenly things, we have invited the peace of Christ to rule in our hearts (vv. 15-17). *The Message* puts it this way:

> Let the peace of Christ keep you in tune with each other, in step with each other. None of this going off and doing your own thing. And cultivate thankfulness. Let the Word of Christ—the Message—have the run of the house. Give it plenty of room in your lives. Instruct and direct one another using good common sense. And sing, sing your hearts out to God! Let every detail in your lives—words, actions, whatever—be done in the name of the Master, Jesus, thanking God the Father every step of the way.

My friend, what Paul is describing is the joyful transformation of our attitudes that comes through worship—when we truly recognize, acknowledge, and focus all we are on the one who is worthy of all praise. J. I. Packer says it so well:

> We need to discover all over again that worship is natural to the Christian, as it was to the godly Israelites who wrote the psalms, and that the habit of celebrating the greatness and graciousness of God yields an endless flow of thankfulness, joy, and zeal.[5]

Thankfulness, joy, and zeal—what a contrast to the all too pervasive attitudes of resentment, anger, and apathy. Our attitudes take root and blossom from where we set our minds and eyes. Where are you looking for truth? What are you thinking about?

A NEW HEART

When we receive the gift of forgiveness and new life, when we truly acknowledge God in worship, we are given a new heart. "I will give you a new heart and put a new spirit in you; I will remove from you your heart of stone and give you a heart of flesh" (Ezekiel 36:26 NIV). That doesn't mean our memories are wiped out. That doesn't mean all consequences of sins committed by us and others disappear—though condemnation from sin is gone. But the engaged heart, the worshiping heart, has a new ability to deal with negative memories and emotions through God's perspective.

We don't suppress the past by pretending it never happened and blocking it from our minds. But our hearts and thoughts choose to focus on the more powerful emotions of being loved and cherished by God, knowing where we will spend eternity, knowing that "the one who is in you is greater than the one who is in the world" (1 John 4:4 NIV), knowing that "in all things God works for the good of those who love him, who have been called according to his purpose" (Romans 8:28 NIV), and knowing that nothing can separate us from the love of God:

> For I am convinced that neither death nor life, neither angels nor demons, neither the present nor the future, nor any powers, neither height nor depth, nor anything else in all creation, will be able to separate us from the love of God that is in Christ Jesus our Lord.
>
> **Romans 8:38-39** NIV

Watch how David turns negative emotions into a joyful declaration:

> O Lord, I have so many enemies;
>> so many are against me.
> So many are saying,
>> "God will never rescue him!"
>
> But you, O Lord, are a shield around me;
>> you are my glory, the one who holds my head high.
> I cried out to the Lord,
>> and he answered me from his holy mountain.
>
> I lay down and slept,
>> yet I woke up in safety,
>> for the Lord was watching over me.
>
> **Psalm 3:1-5**

ON PURPOSE

Let's face it, there is enough negativity in the world today to fill us all with despair, no matter how peaceful our past and present are. So many are drawn to dwell on all that is hopeless and sorrowful. I believe that is a trap set by Satan to steal our joy and keep us from worship.

I would encourage you to listen to God's voice to direct you in this crucial area of your life. If He tells you to turn off a certain television program—even if it is the nightly news—do it. If He tells you one of your favorite musicians is flooding your emotions with negative energy, stop listening. I know how hard this must sound, but yes, you may even need to limit contact or cut off contact with certain people that fill your heart with damaging and crippling thoughts.

Don't think for a second you are being deprived or losing out. There are times when even Jesus had to pull away from negativity to be able to do the Father's will. God's ways are paths of peace. Paul tells us to turn from the negative and dwell on what is positive and beautiful and true:

> Always be full of joy in the Lord. I say it again—rejoice! Let everyone see that you are considerate in all you do. Remember, the Lord is coming soon. Don't worry about anything; instead, pray about everything. Tell God what you need, and thank him for all he has done. Then you will experience God's peace, which exceeds anything we can understand. His peace will guard your hearts and minds as you live in Christ Jesus. And now, dear brothers and sisters, one final thing. Fix your thoughts on what is true, and honorable, and right, and pure, and lovely, and admirable. Think about things that are excellent and worthy of praise.
>
> **Philippians 4:4-8**

David was so poetic, and his psalms are filled with such imagery. But he could also be very plainspoken. His prayer in

Psalm 51:8 was, "Tune me in to foot-tapping songs, set these once-broken bones to dancing" (THE MESSAGE).

Notice that all of this is dependent upon God's grace, but all of it is done on purpose. The set of our minds, our actions, our words are an obedient response to what God has asked of us. Why do I love worship and find such joy there? God called me to it.

> Shout to the Lord, all the earth;
> break out in praise and sing for joy!
> Sing your praise to the Lord with the harp,
> with the harp and melodious song,
> with trumpets and the sound of the ram's horn.
> Make a joyful symphony before the Lord, the King!

Psalm 98:4-6

What has God called you to do? What thoughts is He asking you to dwell on? Whom is He asking you to forgive? What words does He want you to speak? John Piper put it this way:

Christ did not die to forgive sinners who go on treasuring anything above seeing and savoring God. And people who would be happy in heaven if Christ were not there, will not be there. The gospel is not a way to get people to heaven; it is a way to get people to God. It's a way of overcoming every obstacle to everlasting joy in God. If we don't want God above all things, we have not been converted by the gospel.[6]

The world will set many obstacles that keep us from experiencing joy in worship. Too much comfort. Too many fears. Too many entertaining distractions. You will have to bring focus and purpose. You will have to choose. Choose to overcome with no compromise. Choose to set your eyes on God, not fake idols. Choose to turn from grievances to the Healer. Choose to listen to what God says is true about life, not what the world says.

I love how the prophet Habakkuk describes his desire to hear God's voice! "I will climb up to my watchtower and stand at my guard post. There I will wait to see what the Lord says and how he will answer my complaint" (Habakkuk 2:1). He describes the discipline and focus of a soldier as he listens to God.

HE WILL KEEP YOU

The clearest way to choose joy is to choose Jesus. As Matthew Henry said, "What think we of Christ? Is He altogether glorious in our eyes, and precious to our hearts? May Christ be our joy, our confidence, our all. May we daily be made more like to Him, and more devoted to His service."[7]

Are your eyes fixed on Jesus?

> Therefore, since we are surrounded by such a great cloud of witnesses, let us throw off everything that hinders and the sin that so easily entangles. And let us run with perseverance the race marked out for us, fixing our eyes on Jesus, the pioneer and perfecter of faith. For the joy set before him he endured the cross, scorning its shame, and sat down at the right hand of the throne of God. Consider him who endured such opposition from sinners, so that you will not grow weary and lose heart.
>
> Hebrews 12:1-3 NIV

Notice the thoughtfulness we are to bring to the renewing of our attitudes. We *throw off* the hindrances, *put aside* the sin that entangles, *set our eyes*, and *consider* Him with our mind, giving Him our full attention. It's all by grace through faith, as we invite the Holy Spirit to empower us into all things new. The race the writer to the Hebrews refers to is not a hundred-meter dash. It is a marathon. It is the duration of your life on earth. His command is to get rid of the distractions and destructions the world has to offer. Put your eyes on Jesus. He is the one who will see you through to the finish line without growing weary and losing heart—but instead with joy.

One of the most precious prayers in the entire Bible comes at the end of the shortest book in the New Testament: Jude. In his letter, Jude, a sold-out servant of Jesus Christ, prays this for the readers—and for us:

> Now all glory to God, who is able to keep you from falling away and will bring you with great joy into his glorious presence without a single fault. All glory to him who alone is God, our Savior through Jesus Christ our Lord. All glory, majesty, power, and authority are his before all time, and in the present, and beyond all time! Amen.
>
> Jude 1:24-25

When we give God all the glory, when we give glory to Him in His majesty, power, and authority, when we glory in our Savior and Lord, when we worship, something incredible and beautiful happens. We are renewed and protected and given great joy, a joy that will accompany us now and straight through to that moment when we are ushered into His presence without fault or blemish.

CHAPTER 11

MY WORDS

Let the words of my mouth and the meditation
of my heart be acceptable in Your sight, O Lord,
my strength and my Redeemer.

PSALM 19:14 NKJV

POISON OR FRUIT

David's prayer in Psalm 19:14 is so lovely and such a lesson for us: My words and thoughts in every walk of life can express worship for God. Words of hope, love, optimism, encouragement, and truth are such an important aspect of my obedient worship to the God who is all worthy that they literally have the power to transform my life and the lives of others. We shouldn't be surprised. Worship changes everything.

Are you worshiping God with your words? Are you experiencing His transforming power? No one teaches on the power of words better than my dear friend Joyce Meyer. Listen to what she has to say:

> I am sure you have heard someone say, "You are going to eat those words." It may sound like a mere phrase to us, but in reality we do eat our words. What we say not only affects others, but it also affects us. Words are wonderful when used in a proper way. They can encourage, edify and give confidence to

123

the hearer. A right word spoken at the right time can actually be life-changing. . . .

We can literally increase our own joy by speaking right words. We can also upset ourselves by talking unnecessarily about our problems or things that have hurt us in relationships. . . .

The words that come out of our mouth go into our own ears as well as other people's, and then they drop down into our soul, where they give us either joy or sadness, peace or upset, depending on the types of words we have spoken. . . . God desires that our spirit be light and free so it can function properly, not heavy and oppressed.

When we understand the power of words and realize that we can choose what we think and speak, our lives can be transformed. . . . We can learn to choose our thoughts, to resist wrong ones and think on good, healthy, and right ones. I have often said, "Where the mind goes, the man follows." And it could also be said that where the mind goes, the mouth follows![1]

Think about that last sentence carefully. Mull it over in your heart and mind. Don't read ahead too quickly. Do you really believe that the words you say can change your life? I do. Because words of blessing and truth are one of the ways we worship our God and honor the others in our world.

My words tell others—and myself—what I believe about God. They tell others what I believe about myself and my life. They reveal my attitude. I want my words to show true worship—exalting the Mighty One—whether I am in front of a thousand leading worship or talking softly to my kids at bedtime or on the phone with a customer service rep who is not understanding my request. I want my words to be aligned with God's truth.

The Message translates Proverbs 18:21 with such power and clarity: "Words kill, words give life; they're either poison or fruit—you choose."

Which do you choose—sweet, nourishing fruit or poison?

George Orwell, author of the chilling political novel *1984*, gave this warning: "But if thought corrupts language, language can also corrupt thought."[2]

I believe that truth was revealed to him.

THE ABUNDANCE OF THE HEART

Jesus tells us, "It's who you are, not what you say and do, that counts. Your true being brims over into true words and deeds" (Luke 6:45 THE MESSAGE). What do your words tell you about the condition of your heart? When I ask for coffee at my favorite shop or handle a stressful business call or correct my child or open up my heart to my husband at the end of the day, what is the quality of my words, my tone, my facial expressions, my gestures? Who do they say I am?

Even when others are not present, my words need to reflect the abundance of praise, thanksgiving, and joy—my worship—present in my heart.

Ultimately, I want to align my words and thoughts with God's words and thoughts. That's why we can't be careless with what we say and express. As important and central and powerful as the power of our words is in Scripture, there seems to be an attitude that they really don't matter. The coarse, crude, and profane are very acceptable in popular culture—and perhaps in some church circles as well. What about in your vocabulary?

Remember Paul's warning in Ephesians 5:4: "Let there be no filthiness nor foolish talk nor crude joking, which are out of place, but instead let there be thanksgiving" (ESV). He knew full well that our words can lift or lower us spiritually. I've seen people who were a little upset begin to speak out boldly as to what was bothering them, only to see that person move from upset to angry to furious. Words are an expression of the abundance of our heart, but they also speak *into* our heart. And into the hearts of others.

I've probably grown more blunt in this season of my life. Directness and confrontation are not sins. There is a time to get to the point. There is a time to disagree. But not out of self-serving anger. It was Paul who taught us, "In your anger do not sin" (Ephesians 4:26 NIV). Our words, especially our tough words, must be spoken from a heart of love with a spirit of encouragement.

What we say can lift or lower us—and others. That's why a heart filled with worship in our moment-by-moment dealings is so important, so that what flows from the mouth is seasoned with grace and love.

When I was going through treatments, there were some people I needed to separate myself from. I don't think they were malicious, but their words were so negative that I found they weakened me physically. I literally had no margin to manage other people's pain and fear. I found that in this period of physical distress, I had to protect myself and my spirit from anything that would distract me from bold faith, from God's presence, and from all that the Word of God promises.

It is good to remind ourselves to ask what impact our words have on others. That is part of the honesty our words demand from us. Sometimes we need to look in the mirror and say, "Mirror, mirror, on the wall, where are my words and thoughts coming from?"

WORDS ARE AN AMPLIFIER

I want to add one more important thought on the power of words to lift or lower. I've already hinted at it, but it needs to be stressed. Words *amplify* what is in our heart.

A little complaint against a dear one gets spoken recklessly and repeatedly until it becomes a torrent of criticism that wounds someone we love. Something little becomes a huge source of divisiveness.

A small untruth is given breath in our words and becomes a serious breach of trust and damaging to our reputation. The little lie didn't *seem* like a big deal. We weren't even trying to gain much from it, but it becomes amplified and puts a haze of suspicion over a relationship.

We repeat a bit of gossip about someone else in the church. Even as we speak it, we say it may not be true and don't say anything to anyone else, but Pandora's box is opened and the lid cannot be shut. What began as something we considered "harmless" content savages a reputation and causes us to bear false witness against a neighbor.

We tease someone about their body, their mannerisms, something embarrassing from their past. Certainly there is space in life for some good-natured teasing, but even when we are joking, we must be careful that something we consider small doesn't magnify into a source of insecurity—and resentment toward us—in someone else's thoughts and words.

Conversely, a small, positive thought about someone's potential that is spoken softly can become a driving force in a young person's success.

We express a word of thanksgiving for something God has done in us—it really wasn't a big deal in our minds—but someone who doesn't know the love of God hears it, and the spark of faith is planted in their heart, leading to a wonderful moment of salvation. We might not even be there to witness that moment when the love of God breaks through, but our small word of faith becomes something huge and powerful and transformational for that person!

The power of words has a butterfly effect. Consider the words of novelist Dean Koontz, speaking as a voice from the world to the truth of Scripture:

Each smallest act of kindness reverberates across great distances and spans of time—affecting lives unknown to the one whose generous spirit was the source of this good echo. Because kindness is passed on and grows each time it's passed, until a simple courtesy becomes an act of selfless courage years later and far away. Likewise, each small meanness, each expression of hatred, each act of evil.[3]

James describes the power of the tongue this way: "A small rudder makes a huge ship turn wherever the pilot chooses to go, even though the winds are strong" (James 3:4).

We are to speak wisely. We are to speak words that show love and honor to our heavenly Father and our fellow travelers on the journey of life.

SPEAKING AND OBEDIENCE

Our words flow from the abundance of our heart, as does our obedience. There are times when speaking is not just praise and thanksgiving, but a dramatic declaration of obedience. That was so evident in the life of Queen Esther.

There is a passage in Esther 4 that has floored me and challenged my decision-making process; it has rallied my heart to action, continuing to echo in my heart and mind:

> Mordecai sent her this message: "Don't think that just because you live in the king's house you're the one Jew who will get out of this alive. If you persist in staying silent at a time like this, help and deliverance will arrive for the Jews from someplace else; but you and your family will be wiped out. Who knows? Maybe you were made queen for just such a time as this."

Esther 4:12–14 The Message

We often focus our attention on the end of that verse, which is so very powerful, but what makes this passage even more powerful is the front half of the verse. Mordecai, Esther's older cousin who has raised her, lets her know the stakes of remaining silent and not speaking boldly what God has put in her heart.

Whether the need that is on your heart right now is personal, whether it is in regard to your family or the body of Christ, whether it is in regard to anything you are facing that draws upon your heart—one thing I am certain of is that you have been positioned on purpose according to God's amazing plan of redemption. After all, in the end we all have been born into this season in history for such a time as this. But if we become daunted by the size of the challenge we face, or are minimized by the culture we live in, or are silenced by fear of man, or make choices that defy our trust in our almighty God, then we make God wait yet again for someone else to say yes to His call.

Esther's life—which God miraculously spared along with the lives of her nation—is a foreshadowing of Paul's words: "Instead, we will speak the truth in love, growing in every way more and more like Christ, who is the head of his body, the church" (Ephesians 4:15).

Dietrich Bonhoeffer was a German pastor during World War II who was dismayed at the rise of Adolf Hitler and the Nazi Party. But he was almost equally dismayed by the silence of the church as the evil the Nazis were perpetuating at home and abroad became clear. Bonhoeffer could not remain silent. Despite being offered escape to America, where he would be spared, he fought for truth and paid the price as a martyr, hung in the prison where he was held.

He had this to say about speaking the truth: "Silence in the face of evil is itself evil: God will not hold us guiltless. Not to speak is to speak. Not to act is to act."[4]

THE SPIRIT SPEAKS FOR ME

I want my words to reflect the heart of God. Who He is and what He says to me. I want people to hear the love of Jesus when they hear me because worshiping Him in Spirit and truth has led to an abundance of wisdom, grace, encouragement, and thanksgiving flooding out of my heart!

I am so grateful that when my words of prayer can't express all I am thinking and feeling, the Holy Spirit prays on my behalf. "In the same way, the Spirit helps us in our weakness. We do not know what we ought to pray for, but the Spirit himself intercedes for us through wordless groans" (Romans 8:26 NIV).

I am so grateful that when I am outside my own culture and there are language and understanding barriers, the Holy Spirit translates for me. "They were completely amazed. 'How can this be?' they exclaimed. 'These people are all from Galilee, and yet we hear them speaking in our own native languages!'" (Acts 2:7–8).

I am so thankful that when God calls me to speak out in obedience, He gives my words power, just as He did for Esther. Peter and John knew this.

> "And now, O Lord, hear their threats, and give us, your servants, great boldness in preaching your word. Stretch out your hand with healing power; may miraculous signs and wonders be done through the name of your holy servant Jesus."
>
> **Acts 4:29-30**

I am so thankful that when I don't know what to say, God literally, miraculously puts words in my mouth as I am obedient. Consider the call of a young man named Jeremiah. He felt too young to be a prophet of the almighty God.

> The word of the Lord came to me, saying, "Before I formed you in the womb I knew you, before you were born I set you apart; I appointed you as a prophet to the nations."
>
> "Alas, Sovereign Lord," I said, "I do not know how to speak; I am too young."
>
> But the Lord said to me, "Do not say, 'I am too young.' You must go to everyone I send you to and say whatever I command you. Do not be afraid of them, for I am with you and will rescue you," declares the Lord.
>
> Then the Lord reached out his hand and touched my mouth and said to me, "I have put my words in your mouth. See, today I appoint you over nations and kingdoms to uproot and tear down, to destroy and overthrow, to build and to plant."
>
> **Jeremiah 1:4-10** NIV

When you don't know what to say, simply obey and let God fill in the blanks with His divine presence! Charles Spurgeon said it right: "We are all, at times, unconscious prophets."[5]

Wow. Think of that. Simply by being obedient with our words, we can speak the future into the life of the church, a brother or sister in Christ, or even our own lives!

I would add one other note on not having the words to express what is in our hearts. The worship leader who has most revealed Jesus to me, King David, adds a psalm he didn't write—we don't know the author, only that it was dedicated to the sons of Korah. It teaches us that language is more than just words. The psalm calls us to express what's in our hearts with everything we have: "Come, everyone! Clap your hands! Shout to God with joyful praise!" (Psalm 47:1).

You already know your hands speak for you at times. To clap your hands is one of the most natural and enthusiastic ways to express joy. Even when we are with people from other countries and languages, clapping is one way in which we are united. Clapping is one of those unique gestures that is part of the universal language. Without a word, with just clapping hands and a beaming face, each of us knows exactly what is being said. When we praise, express joy, and worship our Great God, our hands join the song. They can't keep still.

Our gestures, posture, tones, volume, and facial expressions communicate so much. That's why the psalmist calls on us to worship with all of our might—clapping and shouting. I know that true worship is not a matter of style, but when I hear the psalmist call for me to clap and shout, you better believe there is going to be shouting and clapping. I find such indescribable joy in the shout of the redeemed. Shouting and clapping is certainly for the church worship service, but the same enthusiasm and spirit are to season all the interactions of my life.

Worship changes everything. That is something to clap about, to shout about, to confess to the world in a joyful song!

SHOUT TO THE LORD

My Jesus, my Savior
Lord, there is none like You
All of my days, I want to praise
The wonders of Your mighty love

My comfort, my shelter
Tower of refuge and strength
Let every breath, all that I am
Never cease to worship You

Shout to the Lord, all the earth, let us sing
Power and majesty, praise to the King
Mountains bow down and the seas will roar
At the sound of Your name

I sing for joy at the work of Your hands
Forever I'll love You, forever I'll stand
Nothing compares to the promise I have
  in You

My Jesus, my Savior
Lord, there is none like You
All of my days, I want to praise
The wonders of Your mighty love

My comfort, my shelter
Tower of refuge and strength
Let every breath, all that I am
Never cease to worship You

Shout to the Lord, all the earth, let us sing
Power and majesty, praise to the King
Mountains bow down and the seas will roar
At the sound of Your name

I sing for joy at the work of Your hands
Forever I'll love You, forever I'll stand
Nothing compares to the promise I have

Shout to the Lord, all the earth, let us sing
Power and majesty, praise to the King
Mountains bow down and the seas will roar
At the sound of Your name

I sing for joy at the work of Your hands
Forever I'll love You, forever I'll stand
Nothing compares to the promise
  I have in You
Nothing compares to the promise
  I have in You
Nothing compares to the promise
  I have in You[6]

CHAPTER 12

SUFFERING

Your most profound and intimate experiences
of worship will likely be in your darkest days—
when your heart is broken, when you feel abandoned,
when you're out of options, when the pain is great,
and you turn to God alone.

RICK WARREN[1]

SUFFERING IS THE REALITY of the world we live in. And I wish
I could tell you that you will never experience suffering yourself.
In the book of Romans, Paul tells us that suffering entered the
world through sin:

> Against its will, all creation was subjected to God's curse. But
> with eager hope, the creation looks forward to the day when
> it will join God's children in glorious freedom from death and
> decay. For we know that all creation has been groaning as in
> the pains of childbirth right up to the present time.
>
> **Romans 8:20-22**

It seems that everywhere we look we find more and more
people truly living under suffering—millions through poverty,
millions through slavery—and yet the beauty of Jesus is that He
always brings *hope*, wherever you are, in whatever circumstance.
Yes, His name is higher than all pain and suffering.

If you are walking through the valley of the shadow of death, all I can say to you today is *hang on*. The psalmist makes a statement that says, "Though darkness is all around, I will fear *no* evil" (see Psalm 23:4).

My heart breaks for my brothers and sisters in Christ who are under persecution, for those who are in abusive relationships, for children who are growing up without loving parents to guide them and instill in them an assurance of being loved. There are those who conspire to tear down our sense of worth and potential. They would have us live with a spirit of fear, intimidation, depression, and oppression. That's why within these chapters on worshiping God in every season, it is critical to remember the finished work of the cross when evil tries to press in on every side. Whatever situation you find yourself in, know this: God is present. Worship Him—recognizing and acknowledging His greatness—even in moments of great pain, and you will discover His grace and power is sufficient: "Three different times I begged the Lord to take it away. Each time he said, 'My grace is all you need. My power works best in weakness'" (2 Corinthians 12:8–9).

SOUL SUFFERING

There is brokenness of body and a brokenness of what is inside us. I believe that soul-spirit-heart suffering makes us the most vulnerable to the attacks of Satan and the weakening of our faith. Solomon describes this brokenness by saying, "The human spirit can endure a sick body, but who can bear a crushed spirit?" (Proverbs 18:14). Have you ever been in a place where the city walls of your spirit, your personhood, have been broken down? Where are you open to attack?

I recently met a girl from a great Christian family. Like so many young women do, she began to compare herself to others, against the impossible standards and images that today's media project for our young people. It wasn't long before self-doubt consumed her, which led to an eating disorder and full-blown rebellion. She became erratic and unemployable, and the overwhelming guilt she felt for disappointing her family finally drove her to run away. From there, things only got worse: She was raped, turned to prostitution, and had two abortions. If not for the love of Jesus and some good Christian friends who refused to judge her or give up on her, she would not be with us today.

Not all situations are that intense, but to be honest, I am never really surprised at what I hear when people open up to me about their lives—we live in a very broken world. Without Him, without God's plan for redemption, we would have no hope.

One of the most dramatic stories of soul suffering in the Bible is Joseph. Perhaps he showed a lack of wisdom in how he shared his dreams with his brothers (see Genesis 37:5-11). Maybe it seemed like bragging the way he let them know in no uncertain terms that they would serve him. Perhaps his father, Jacob, was not wise in showing such favoritism to Joseph over his brothers with the gift of a beautiful coat (vv. 3-4). But no one deserves to be mistreated as he was by family. He was beaten and his coat was ripped off him. His brothers dipped it in blood as proof that he was killed by wild animals. He was thrown in a pit. He was sold as a slave. He was abused by his brothers, the ones who should have been his protectors—even if he was the lippy younger brother.

Some of the deepest suffering of life is not of body, but of spirit. Joseph knew that well. He knew both kinds of suffering, but as he languished in an Egyptian prison—another experience of betrayal and abuse for him—my thought is that his heart wounds caused him more suffering than his bodily wounds ever could have.

GET OUT OF THAT PIT

When you are in the pit of suffering, there is only one direction you can go: up. Look up. Look for God. Look for your Redeemer. We know that's what Joseph did when he told his brothers why he forgave them (after testing their character): "You intended to harm me, but God intended it all for good. He brought me to this position so I could save the lives of many people" (Genesis 50:20). He saw God's hand at work in his life. He never doubted God's love for him. He knew that even if he had lost his lovely multicolored coat, the sign of his earthly father's favor, he was favored by God—his heavenly Father—and that he still had a part in God's plan to save His people. Like Esther, he knew he was born for this moment and had an eternal destiny.

This chapter on worshiping God in our suffering is incredibly important to me. Mark and I have come through the hardest year of our lives. My life has not been without challenges beginning in childhood, but honestly, I have felt so protected in my days and years. Breast cancer was a new level of deep suffering. My theology was put through a sieve, and I had to lean into every Scripture I knew to be true about God's providence, and that it was not His desire that I or my family should suffer. To see His kids in pain hurts Him too. To fully trust God during times of immense pain is one of the great gifts of a trial. You find the beautiful Holy Spirit is there, no matter how broken you are or how disappointed you are or how hopeless you feel. To rediscover these words in Galatians was a real strength to me:

> But the fruit of the [Holy] Spirit [the work which His presence within accomplishes] is love, joy (gladness), peace, patience (an even temper, forbearance), kindness, goodness (benevolence), faithfulness, gentleness (meekness, humility), self-control (self-restraint, continence). Against such things there is no law [that can bring a charge].
>
> Galatians 5:22-23 Amplified

The fruit of the spirit gives us the ability to stand—not our human energy, or lack thereof.

David and Joseph, my heroes of faith, were inspiring to me during this time. They walked through many paths of suffering, some from the hands of loved ones, some from the battles of life, some from their own doing. Suffering comes to us as part of life, at the hands of others, and yes, as part of our own decisions, but sometimes just because we live in this fallen world. Our bodies break down, accidents happen, war and famine continue. Yes, suffering is part of our human experience. But follow David's conversation with God:

> As the deer longs for streams of water,
>> so I long for you, O God.
> I thirst for God, the living God.
>> When can I go and stand before him?
> Day and night I have only tears for food,
>> while my enemies continually taunt me, saying,
>> "Where is this God of yours?"
>
> My heart is breaking
>> as I remember how it used to be:
> I walked among the crowds of worshipers,
>> leading a great procession to the house of God,
> singing for joy and giving thanks
>> amid the sound of a great celebration!
>
> Why am I discouraged?
>> Why is my heart so sad?
> I will put my hope in God!
>> I will praise him again—
>> my Savior and my God!
>
> Now I am deeply discouraged,
>> but I will remember you—
> even from distant Mount Hermon, the source of the Jordan,
>> from the land of Mount Mizar.
> I hear the tumult of the raging seas
>> as your waves and surging tides sweep over me.
> But each day the Lord pours his unfailing love upon me,
>> and through each night I sing his songs,
>> praying to God who gives me life.
>
> "O God my rock," I cry,
>> "Why have you forgotten me?

Why must I wander around in grief,
 oppressed by my enemies?"
Their taunts break my bones.
 They scoff, "Where is this God of yours?"

Why am I discouraged?
 Why is my heart so sad?
I will put my hope in God!
 I will praise him again—
 my Savior and my God.

Psalm 42

 Wounded and beat down. At the end of his rope. Feeling utterly forsaken and forgotten—even by God. Every dream appeared to be nothing more than smoldering ashes. Friends were enemies. But what does he do?

- David looked up—he hungered and thirsted for God with a physical desperation. He never lost his trust in God's love and faithfulness; even in his darkest moments he knew God was present. God is always present. He is *very present* in our time of troubles! "God is our refuge and strength, a *very present* help in trouble!" (Psalm 46:1 NKJV, emphasis added).

- He was honest about his hurts and his feelings before God. Some fear that pouring our thoughts and emotions out to God will make Him stop loving us or offend Him and drive Him from our lives or show disrespect and lack of reverence. First of all, He is all-knowing and already knows what is in your heart and mind. Second, He tells us to bring all our cares and troubles to Him. Third, He wants us to be honest. Bring your doubts, fears, hurts, and anger before God. He is mighty and powerful. He's got broad shoulders. He can handle anything you throw at Him, including your honesty.

- David remembered the faithfulness of God and how God had delivered him before. All throughout Scripture there are commands to remember—to forget not. This is repeated more than four hundred times! The children of Israel were to remember God's deliverance from slavery in many different ways, but especially the Feast of the Passover. As Christians we are to remember our freedom from the slavery of sin when we gather for communion. Count your blessings and remember God's gracious activity in your life. That is exactly what David did when he said, "I will remember you."

- He claimed the power of hope and sealed it with praise—declaring the worthiness of God to be trusted and worshiped. "I will put my hope in God! I will praise him again—my Savior and my God." When you are in the pit of despair and look up to see the face of God, praise Him!

- He sang. Oh how I sang during my hardest moments. Oh how I had to learn to worship during chemo. Oh the power of a song of praise and love! I have a special playlist that I am so grateful for. It was the songs that brought peace and comfort to my body and spirit. When you don't know what to do about your pain and situation, sing!

- He experienced healing in the depths of his spirit: "I hear the tumult of the raging seas as your waves and surging tides sweep over me. But each day the Lord pours his unfailing love upon me."

David shows us how the heart of worship is the only true road to healing from our past and overcoming any present suffering—physical, emotional, or otherwise.

FORGIVENESS

When your hurt and suffering comes at the hand of someone else, your healing and peace will be based on your forgiveness. I have seen too many people who have tried to hurt someone else to get revenge, not forgiving them. Withholding forgiveness doesn't bother some evildoers, but one way or another it always ends up hurting the one who holds on to bitterness. It inhibits the flow of God's grace in our lives. The Lord's Prayer teaches us the importance of God's forgiveness to us and our forgiveness to others: "Forgive us our sins, as we have forgiven those who sin against us" (Matthew 6:12). Refusing to forgive keeps us connected to the one who hurt us and tied to our pain and suffering. Paul tells us to forget the past and move on.

A young girl was sexually abused by her grandfather. As an adult, she went to a Christian counselor who let her know that freedom would only come through forgiveness. She took his words to heart and traveled to confront and forgive her grandfather. She did not say anything in front of her grandmother. She took a drive with him. She stopped the car, reminded him of what he had done to her, and told him she forgave him through the love of Jesus. She reported her story to her counselor, who was impressed and amazed.

"How did he respond?" he asked.

"He laughed and made a sexual pass at me."

"What did you do?!"

"I told him I could not see him again, but that I still forgave him through the love of Jesus."

That's healing. That's worship.

In the Sermon on the Mount, Jesus tells us, "But I say, love your enemies! Pray for those who persecute you!" (Matthew 5:44). Notice what happens as we draw close to God and become more like Him—we can even pray for our enemies! That's attacking our suffering at the root.

NO MATTER WHAT THE CIRCUMSTANCES

The stance of worship is made possible only through the power of the Holy Spirit. We worship Him in our moments of success. But we also worship Him in suffering, when we are in the wilderness.

Job lost everything he had and faced more hurt and hardship in two afternoons than most of us will experience in a lifetime—livestock stolen, crops burned, home destroyed, and then the ultimate blow: his seven precious children killed. He sat in the ashes in abject misery, but he refused to not worship. "God might kill me, but I have no other hope. I am going to argue my case with him. But this is what will save me—I am not godless. If I were, I could not stand before him" (Job 13:15-16).

Paul was beaten, stoned, rejected, and put in prison many times for his bold, fearless faith that proclaimed the good news of Jesus Christ. He didn't focus on circumstances but set his eyes on the mighty God who is worthy of all praise. It was in a Philippian jail where an incredible, miraculous worship service broke out that revealed the power of God and brought salvation to an entire family. It began with Paul being brought before the city elders on trumped-up charges. We then read:

> The judges went along with the mob, had Paul and Silas's clothes ripped off and ordered a public beating. After beating them black-and-blue, they threw them into jail, telling the jailkeeper to put them under heavy guard so there would be no chance of escape. He did just that—threw them into the maximum security cell in the jail and clamped leg irons on them.
>
> Along about midnight, Paul and Silas were at prayer and singing a robust hymn to God. The other prisoners couldn't believe their ears. Then, without warning, a huge earthquake! The jailhouse tottered, every door flew open, all the prisoners were loose.
>
> Startled from sleep, the jailer saw all the doors swinging loose on their hinges. Assuming that all the prisoners had escaped, he pulled out his sword and was about to do himself in, figuring he was as good as dead anyway, when Paul stopped him: "Don't do that! We're all still here! Nobody's run away!"
>
> The jailer got a torch and ran inside. Badly shaken, he collapsed in front of Paul and Silas. He led them out of the jail and

asked, "Sirs, what do I have to do to be saved, to really live?" They said, "Put your entire trust in the Master Jesus. Then you'll live as you were meant to live—and everyone in your house included!"

Acts 16:22-31 THE MESSAGE

One of the great prophets of God to His people, Elijah, went through a series of events that brought him to his knees to the point where he was ready to commit suicide. His emotions took a roller coaster ride, from the exaltation of proving the one true God (see 1 Kings 18:16-40) to being hunted down by a vengeful queen (see 19:1-3). His suffering turned to depression to the point that he wanted to die (v. 4). But he turned his ear to God and received just what he needed in a still small voice (v. 12). God even used ravens to feed him (17:2-4).

Worship is expressed in many ways, such as our enthusiastic love, praise, and giving to God. But sometimes, and critically so, it is expressed by being silent and listening for Him. Proverbs 3:5-12 from *The Message* says this:

> Trust God from the bottom of your heart;
>> don't try to figure out everything on your own.
> Listen for God's voice in everything you do, everywhere
>> you go;
>> he's the one who will keep you on track.
> Don't assume that you know it all.
>> Run to God! Run from evil!
> Your body will glow with health,
>> your very bones will vibrate with life!
> Honor God with everything you own;
>> give him the first and the best.
> Your barns will burst,
>> your wine vats will brim over.
> But don't, dear friend, resent God's discipline;
>> don't sulk under his loving correction.
> It's the child he loves that God corrects;
>> a father's delight is behind all this.

When you really have to trust God, your relationship with Him is of the utmost importance. Like any relationship that is strengthened through time and conversation, knowing God's voice when He speaks to you and then following His direction always leads to a deeper intimacy with Him.

How do we hear from God? He is speaking to us all the time. We need to be people who know how to be still and wait upon Him. He speaks through His Word. He speaks as we worship. He speaks to our spirit as we pray and listen to His voice. Some people walk and pray and listen; others, like me, open the Word and worship and play an instrument; some go to a sacred place where they love to meet with God. Whatever it is, the anointing of the Holy Spirit is faithful to teach and instruct us, as long as we are willing to listen.

Are you suffering? In pain? Discover God's grace in worship. Be honest, but listen. Look up. Take to heart Paul's words: "No, despite all these things, overwhelming victory is ours through Christ, who loved us" (Romans 8:37).

NO ONE LIKE YOU

There's no one like Jesus
There's no one like Jesus
Rescued me from darkness
Fill my life with gladness
Carrying my burdens
Peace in every battle
There's no one like Jesus
Calm in every storm

You walk with me through suffering
You will not let me go
Your presence overwhelms my heart
Lord there's no one like You

There's no one like Jesus
There's no one like Jesus
Strength in times of weakness
Joyful in Your presence
You meet me in my sadness
Walk with me through fire
There's no one like Jesus
Calm in every storm

You won it all at Calvary
The saving grace of God
I'll never be the same again
Lord there's no one like You

The heavens are open over me
Your glory is like the sun
And nothing can separate me
From Your love[2]

CHAPTER 13

MONEY

"No one can serve two masters.
For you will hate one and love the other;
you will be devoted to one and despise the other.
You cannot serve both God and money."

MATTHEW 6:24

MONEY IS A REVEALER. Your thoughts, attitudes, and actions about money will say much about your character—and your thoughts about God—from your beliefs about His nature to your trust in His goodness.

Billy Graham says, "If a person gets his attitude toward money straight, it will help straighten out almost every other area of his life."[1] Worship and money go hand in hand. The second commandment says, "You must not make for yourself an idol of any kind or an image of anything in the heavens or on the earth or in the sea" (Exodus 20:4). When Jesus says we cannot serve "two masters," He is clearly showing that money is a powerful force that can turn our hearts from worship of God to worship of gold.

But money also becomes a golden opportunity to reveal and magnify our absolute trust in God—that God is owner and giver of all we have and need. Money provides an opportunity for us to give God all the glory for owning everything and graciously meeting all our needs. Money is a golden opportunity to worship!

Jesus is not negative about money for its own sake—but for our sake. He wants to know who is lord of our lives. He wants our thoughts, our attitudes, our words, and our behavior with money to acknowledge His goodness, to recognize that He alone is the source of all good things.

THE CREATOR OWNS ALL

David was able to paint pictures of God and who He is and what He does from images drawn from his own experiences. His years as a shepherd, outdoors in the beauty of God's creation, gave him a glimpse of God's house and God's possessions: in other words, *everything*! This man after God's heart understood that God was the source of all provision: "For all the animals of the forest are mine, and I own the cattle on a thousand hills" (Psalm 50:10). "The earth is the Lord's, and everything in it. The world and all its people belong to him. For he laid the earth's foundation on the seas and built it on the ocean depths" (Psalm 24:1-2).

This is not just David's theme and testimony. All throughout Scripture, we read that God created all, is in all, and owns all. As Moses leads the people of Israel from slavery in Egypt toward the Promised Land, he speaks God's word. He is the owner and giver all good things: "Now if you will obey me and keep my covenant, you will be my own special treasure from among all the peoples on earth; for all the earth belongs to me" (Exodus 19:5). Later Moses reminds his people who had still not learned the lessons of trust and obedience to the Provider God: "Look, the highest heavens and the earth and everything in it all belong to the Lord your God" (Deuteronomy 10:14). As Job, a man who had lost everything, reasons with God, he hears this divine reminder in his heart: "Who has given me anything that I need to pay back? Everything under heaven is mine" (Job 41:11).

Paul puts in vividly clear perspective the difference between trusting money and trusting God as the source of joy, peace, and contentment when he reminds his protégé Timothy:

A devout life does bring wealth, but it's the rich simplicity of being yourself before God. Since we entered the world penniless and will leave it penniless, if we have bread on the table and shoes on our feet, that's enough.

But if it's only money these leaders are after, they'll self-destruct in no time. Lust for money brings trouble and nothing but trouble. Going down that path, some lose their footing in the faith completely and live to regret it bitterly ever after.

But you, Timothy, man of God: Run for your life from all this. Pursue a righteous life—a life of wonder, faith, love, steadiness, courtesy. Run hard and fast in the faith. Seize the eternal life, the life you were called to, the life you so fervently embraced in the presence of so many witnesses.

1 Timothy 6:6-12 THE MESSAGE

Worship is putting God first and acknowledging that God owns all. Anything we have is given by Him for us to manage as stewards. The fabulous news is that God is so generous with His people—with you and me—that we can be content with much or little, knowing He meets our every need abundantly. David declares the earth is full of the loving-kindness of the Lord (see Psalm 33:5).

Mark and I have spoken to so many people in developing nations who live among much suffering and who tell us story after story of incredible and miraculous provision day after day as God himself provides water, food, and most of all, hope. Even when we do not see a way forward, God himself is working *all* things together for good for those who love Him and are called according to His purpose.

From the very beginning of time, God has been gracious and generous with us, for we are His beloved. God did not give Adam and Eve a desert to live in—He gave them a lush, fruitful garden. It was a place of provision and beauty and wealth! "Then the Lord God planted a garden. . . . The Lord God made all sorts of trees grow up from the ground—trees that were beautiful and that produced delicious fruit." Read through Genesis 2 again if you doubt even for a second that God is good and generous to His people. Even after the fall, even after Adam and Eve were expelled from the garden because of disobedience, He continues to be the provider of all that we need. What a beautiful affirmation from Paul when he says, "And this same God who takes care of me will supply all your needs from his glorious riches, which have been given to us in Christ Jesus" (Philippians 4:19).

David brings us back to the heart of worship—acknowledging God, calling to God, praising God—and shows the connection between God's provision and our praise. Throughout Psalm 34 David blesses God's name as his provider. Lions might go hungry, but not those who seek God with their hearts.

> I will praise the Lord at all times.
>> I will constantly speak his praises.
> I will boast only in the Lord;
>> let all who are helpless take heart.
> Come, let us tell of the Lord's greatness;
>> let us exalt his name together.
>
> I prayed to the Lord, and he answered me.
>> He freed me from all my fears.
> Those who look to him for help will be radiant with joy;
>> no shadow of shame will darken their faces.
> In my desperation I prayed, and the Lord listened;
>> he saved me from all my troubles.
> For the angel of the Lord is a guard;
>> he surrounds and defends all who fear him.
>
> Taste and see that the Lord is good.
>> Oh, the joys of those who take refuge in him!
> Fear the Lord, you his godly people,
>> for those who fear him will have all they need.
> Even strong young lions sometimes go hungry,
>> but those who trust in the Lord will lack
>> no good thing.

Psalm 34:1-10

There is so much to digest: praise Him at all times; boast only in the Lord, exalt His name; I prayed, He listened; taste and see that the Lord is good; those who fear Him will have everything they need; they will lack no good thing.

This psalm is such an incredible expression of worship because it wraps together our praise and our trust and our acknowledgment of God's goodness. Worshiping God with our finances starts there. Praise God for His faithful provision. Check your heart right now. Where is your trust and hope?

LET IT GO

If you have clung to possessions as something you own and control, let go now. Worship. Affirm God as the owner and giver of all: "Whatever is good and perfect is a gift coming down to us from God our Father, who created all the lights in the heavens" (James 1:17). Don't let God's gift of money rob you of joy and faith. James warned the wealthy,

> Look here, you rich people: Weep and groan with anguish because of all the terrible troubles ahead of you. Your wealth is rotting away, and your fine clothes are moth-eaten rags. Your gold and silver are corroded. The very wealth you were counting on will eat away your flesh like fire. This corroded treasure you have hoarded will testify against you on the day of judgment.
>
> James 5:1-3

When your trust is in money, it becomes an idol. The very blessing God has given to meet your needs, the needs of advancing His kingdom, and the needs of others out of your abundance becomes a source of worry and fear.

Jesus confronts and comforts us to not let money become our focus:

> What I'm trying to do here is get you to relax, not be so preoccupied with *getting*, so you can respond to God's *giving*. People

who don't know God and the way he works fuss over these things, but you know both God and how he works. Steep yourself in God-reality, God-initiative, God-provisions. You'll find all your everyday human concerns will be met. Don't be afraid of missing out. You're my dearest friends! The Father wants to give you the very kingdom itself. Be generous. Give to the poor. Get yourselves a bank that can't go bankrupt, a bank in heaven far from bankrobbers, safe from embezzlers, a bank you can bank on. It's obvious, isn't it? The place where your treasure is, is the place you will most want to be, and end up being.

Luke 12:29-34 The Message

When we find our identity and hope in anything other than God, the very thing that we think will bring us comfort and peace will rob us of those things. Let go. Don't grasp. Don't worry. Acknowledge God. Trust God—not your possessions.

Charles Swindoll counsels:

We're back to where we started: God owns it all. You will never be in financial trouble if you remember those four words. They will revolutionize your thinking on finances. I wish "God owns it all" could appear on every checkbook, every pocketbook, every income tax return, every stock transaction, every credit card, every home mortgage, every car title, every real estate contract, and every business deal. I wish all the stuff in our homes—including our houses—were stamped with that reminder in bold letters.[2]

God owns it all. Let those words sink deep into your spirit and soul. Write it down. Underline it. Speak it until you believe it with all your heart!

Money is not evil. But love of money is. When it becomes your security, your passion, your center, you are no longer in the spirit of worship. Scripture is filled with warnings that when money gets out of perspective, it shipwrecks our faith.

J. C. Ryle said, "Nothing I am sure has such a tendency to quench the fire of religion as the possession of money."[3] John Chrysostom, an early church father, said, "A dreadful thing is the love of money! It disables both eyes and ears, and makes men worse to deal with than a wild beast, allowing a man to consider neither conscience nor friendship nor fellowship nor salvation."[4]

The solution is not to condemn money but to worship God in the way we view and use money. Rick Warren says, "Most people fail to realize that money is both a *test* and a *trust* from God."[5] If you think back to the words of Paul to Timothy that we shared earlier, Paul begins his statement with "A devout life brings wealth." Can we assume from this that God will bless us and use those blessings to bring us to a point of clarity and deliberate, conscious worship?

I believe so. God blesses so generously but asks us to honor Him with these gifts by not falling into the trap of self-sufficiency but remaining firmly reliant on God; by not letting money turn us into selfish misers but to give back through our tithes and offerings; by being generous in all things; by not finding our identity in what we have or don't have but in our relationship with Him; by not taking blessings for granted but by thanking Him always and in all circumstances.

How we steward money is a tangible way to affirm our belief that God is great and God is good.

In a poignant moment in Jesus' life and ministry, He meets a wealthy young man. This "rich young ruler" catches our Lord's attention. We are told Jesus felt love for him. Perhaps He spotted someone who could become a powerful minister in establishing His kingdom on earth. The man was drawn to Jesus as well. He recognized something unique and compelling in Jesus' life and teaching. He affirmed that he devoutly followed all the commandments and wanted to know if he was missing anything.

Jesus said, "Yes. Give everything you have to the poor." Jesus was asking him the fundamental question of what he truly loved, trusted, and worshiped—"Is it God or money for you?" The man froze. It was his moment of truth. And he walked away. It broke Jesus' heart to see someone with so much spiritual potential grasp tightly to a gift from God rather than God himself. Notice how the short encounter ends:

> Looking at him, Jesus felt a love for him and said to him, "One thing you lack: go and sell all you possess and give to the poor, and you will have treasure in heaven; and come, follow Me." But at these words he was saddened, and he went away grieving, for he was one who owned much property.

> Mark 10:21-22 NASB

I'm sure he was a good man. I'm sure he gave to others. He just didn't have the faith to acknowledge that everything he had was owned by God and given as a gift from Him. What a personal tragedy, but one that is all too common today. John was speaking to a first-century church—but also to us—when he said, "You say, 'I am rich. I have everything I want. I don't need a thing!' And you don't realize that you are wretched and miserable and poor and blind and naked" (Revelation 3:17).

Money is a revealer and a magnifier. It will magnify our faith—or magnify our foolishness. Solomon reminds us in Ecclesiastes 5:10, "Those who love money will never have enough. How meaningless to think that wealth brings true happiness!" The arrogance of self-sufficiency is foolish. Paul reminds Timothy,

> Teach those who are rich in this world not to be proud and not to trust in their money, which is so unreliable. Their trust should be in God, who richly gives us all we need for our enjoyment. Tell them to use their money to do good. They should be rich in good works and generous to those in need, always being ready to share with others. By doing this they will be storing up their treasure as a good foundation for the future so that they may experience true life.

> 1 Timothy 6:17-19

BLESSED AND A BLESSING

When God called the father of our faith, Abraham, He established the principle that we are always blessed to be a blessing:

> The Lord had said to Abram, "Leave your native country, your relatives, and your father's family, and go to the land that I will show you. I will make you into a great nation. I will bless you and make you famous, and you will be a blessing to others. I will bless those who bless you and curse those who treat you with contempt. All the families on earth will be blessed through you."
>
> **Genesis 12:1-3**

God blesses us to bless others, in our talents, our gifts, and our money. Pastor and theologian John Piper puts it strongly:

> The person who thinks the money he makes is meant mainly to increase his comforts on earth is a fool, Jesus says. Wise people know that all their money belongs to God and should be used to show that God, and not money, is their treasure, their comfort, their joy, and their security.[6]

I love the way the great English thinker and writer George MacDonald put it:

> But for money and the need of it, there would not be half the friendship in the world. It is powerful for good when divinely used. Give it plenty of air, and it is sweet as the hawthorn; shut it up and it cankers and breeds worms.[7]

How do you keep wealth from choking out the seed of faith? You worship God as you bless others. You set it free—knowing that there is more where that came from in God's divine economy. You give generously with a joyful spirit, and it becomes worship. Paul proclaims that God delights in a joyful giver (see 2 Corinthians 9:7).

Is it any wonder the early church spread explosively across the Roman Empire? The followers of Christ loved each other so deeply that no one went without. They blessed joyfully. They took care of each other as worship to God and a witness to His love in their world.

Worship changes everything—including wealth. When we stop serving money and let our money serve God, we are free from the bondage of worldly pursuits.

We begin to experience the miracle of God opening the windows of heaven, as is described in this beautiful passage in Malachi 3:10 (NIV):

> "Bring the whole tithe into the storehouse, that there may be food in my house. Test me in this," says the Lord Almighty, "and see if I will not throw open the floodgates of heaven and pour out so much blessing that there will not be room enough to store it."

Will you believe the word of the Lord given to Malachi? Will you believe the further testimony of Paul?

> Remember: A stingy planter gets a stingy crop; a lavish planter gets a lavish crop. I want each of you to take plenty of time to think it over, and make up your own mind what you will give. That will protect you against sob stories and arm-twisting. God loves it when the giver delights in the giving.
>
> God can pour on the blessings in astonishing ways so that you're ready for anything and everything, more than just ready to do what needs to be done. As one psalmist puts it,
>
>> He throws caution to the winds,
>>> giving to the needy in reckless abandon.
>> His right living, right-giving ways
>>> never run out, never wear out.

This most generous God who gives seed to the farmer that becomes bread for your meals is more than extravagant with you. He gives you something you can then give away, which grows into full-formed lives, robust in God, wealthy in every way, so that you can be generous in every way, producing with us great praise to God.

2 Corinthians 9:6–14 The Message

HOW MUCH?

I've got this much. How much is for me? How much for God? How much for others?

C. S. Lewis said,

I do not believe one can settle how much we ought to give. I am afraid the only safe rule is to give more than we can spare. In other words, if our expenditure on comforts, luxuries, amusements, etc., is up to the standard common among those with the same income as our own, we are probably giving away too little. If our charities do not at all pinch or hamper us, I should say they are too small. There ought to be things we should like to do and cannot do because our charitable expenditures exclude them.[8]

Fulton Sheen said, "Never measure your generosity by what you give, but rather by what you have left."[9]

Does that mean I worship God by giving until it hurts? When our use of money is worship of God, it happens entirely differently. We don't give until it hurts. We simply live to give. The question is no longer how much but rather what does God want you to do? Let Him lead by His Spirit.

The story of Jesus observing the gift of a poor widow reveals such a pure act of worship with money.

Just then he looked up and saw the rich people dropping offerings in the collection plate. Then he saw a poor widow put in two pennies. He said, "The plain truth is that this widow has given by far the largest offering today. All these others made offerings that they'll never miss; she gave extravagantly what she couldn't afford—she gave her all!"

Luke 21:1-4 THE MESSAGE

Her extravagant gift so moved the heart of our Lord that He couldn't let the moment pass without bringing it to His disciples' attention. "Look! Did you see that? Don't miss what just happened." Their eyes and ears were quite likely drawn to the rich who were dropping handfuls of loud clanging coins in the offering plate. Jesus' eyes were drawn to worship.

A beautiful lady once gave me an authentic ancient "widow's mite" in a small blue jewelry box, which I keep at my desk to remind me constantly of Jesus' priorities in worship.

Giving back to God anything and everything—knowing full well it is His to begin with and He will always reward our devotion—was a hard lesson for the disciples to grasp when Mary anointed Jesus' feet in an act of adoration:

When Jesus was at Bethany, a guest of Simon the Leper, a woman came up to him as he was eating dinner and anointed him with a bottle of very expensive perfume. When the disciples saw what was happening, they were furious. "That's criminal! This could have been sold for a lot and the money handed out to the poor."

When Jesus realized what was going on, he intervened. "Why are you giving this woman a hard time? She has just done something wonderfully significant for me. You will have the poor with you every day for the rest of your lives, but not me. When she poured this perfume on my body, what she really did was anoint me for burial. You can be sure that wherever in the whole world the Message is preached, what she has just done is going to be remembered and admired."

Matthew 26:6-13 THE MESSAGE

Mary worshiped Jesus with her gift. Did she know she was anointing His body for burial? Probably not. Did she do it knowing her story of lavish devotion would still be shared centuries later? Definitely not. She simply loved and worshiped her Lord.

The gift made no sense to the disciples, and they were angry—despite Jesus' earlier life lesson on how pleased God was with the widow who gave two pennies. Before we judge them too harshly, we must let God's light shine in our own hearts and actions. What is our relationship with money? Martin Luther, a great reformer in church history, provided such a clever, deeply insightful quip on this: "People go through three conversions: their head, their heart, and their pocketbook. Unfortunately, not all at the same time."[10]

As you read further in Matthew 26, you will witness Judas Iscariot leaving directly from this dinner to meet with the chief priests and plot the betrayal of his Lord. What a tragedy. And what a poignant reminder of the seductive power of money to lead us into sin.

But the widow and the former harlot provide poignant reminders of worship by giving so much with such love and devotion and instant obedience. Judas' greed led him to destruction. Their generosity freed them from worry and made them rich!

How much should you give? I can't answer that. It's between you and God. But I know the all-encompassing answer for all of life is we give everything to God. Your whole being. All that you have and all that you are. Place your heart before God, and He will let you enjoy all you need in abundance. "Wherever your treasure is, there the desires of your heart will also be" (Matthew 6:21).

John Wesley's simple formula for money[11] is a wonderful blueprint when practiced in the spirit of worship:

Make all you can—God truly does bring prosperity to the righteous.

Save all you can—Mr. Wesley was speaking specifically of not being wasteful: Don't throw money away on things that don't matter. "The good man's earnings advance the cause of righteousness. The evil man squanders his on sin" (Proverbs 10:16 TLB).

Give all you can—with a cheerful heart, knowing that your gift is worship for your Lord and Savior.

CHAPTER 14

LOVING MYSELF

You made all the delicate, inner parts of my body
and knit me together in my mother's womb.
Thank you for making me so wonderfully complex!
Your workmanship is marvelous — how well I know it.

PSALM 139:13-14

I LOVE TEACHING from the life of Esther. Esther was a beautiful young Jewish girl. An orphan, she was raised by her devout relative Mordecai in the city of Susa, what was then the capital of the Persian Empire.

Esther became bride to King Ahasuerus in what can only be considered bloody circumstances. Ahasuerus got drunk and ugly at a week-long feast. He ordered his then bride, Queen Vashti, to appear before him and his equally drunk and ugly friends in her crown—some scholars believe his command was that she wear *only* her crown. She refused. To set an example to any other women in his kingdom who might think it was acceptable to refuse her husband's demands, no matter how boorish and demeaning, he had Queen Vashti executed.

To find his new queen, Ahasuerus decided to hold a year-long beauty pageant. Beautiful young virgins were brought to the palace and went through a regimen to make them their most attractive selves. At the end of the year, Ahasuerus chose the young Jewish orphan, born with the name Hadassah but known to us as Esther.

159

When teaching this subject one day at one of our Sisters gatherings, I asked them to repeat after me: *"I am loved and cherished by God!"* Every woman in the room confidently repeated that phrase. No hesitation. I then asked them to repeat after me: *"God can accomplish great works through me!"* All the women repeated the phrase, though not quite as quickly and boldly. I then asked them to repeat: *"God has created me absolutely beautiful!"* The response became awkward. With encouragement, every woman repeated the words, but there was nervous laughter and much less gusto.

I know that physical beauty is subjective and relative, but I suspect for many precious women all over the planet, their feelings about their outward beauty are a reflection of how they—and many of us—feel about our inward beauty.

Queen Esther—born an orphan, living in a land that was often hostile to her people, given a new name so she would fit in—was now married to a man who was willing to kill a loved one if he or she crossed him. I'm not so sure how beautiful she felt on the inside, even if she would be a Miss Universe finalist today. She was not loved for who she was but for what she was to him.

We know how the story unfolds. How could this young woman in such a precarious position stand up to a bully? How could she cross him or displease him? But that was exactly what was required if she was to take a bold step of obedience to save the lives of her people. Her uncle came to her in desperation. The king had been manipulated into killing her people by Haman, a man who hated the Jews, the foreigners, living in Susa. Knowing what happened to Vashti, there could be no doubt in Esther's mind that if she opposed Ahasuerus, her husband would kill her.

I believe Esther's bold stand was empowered by all those godly words Mordecai had instilled in her, as she was prepared on the inside for this important moment. She truly mattered. She was significant. She just had to keep on doing the right thing. She was born for this moment.

Do you know how wonderful you are? Do you know your true value—how much you are truly worth?

You are more precious than any outward accomplishment or possession. God declares you priceless! One day while walking with friends into a slum in India, we were asked if we wanted to buy a girl outright (for life) for eight dollars. It's hard to imagine the absolute rejection many people feel because they have a pathetic price put on their heads by others, by society, and sometimes by family. This is *so* opposite to the heart of God for each one of us.

AGREEING WITH GOD

When we worship God, we align our hearts, wills, and thoughts with His heart, will, and thoughts. How can we love our neighbor as we love ourselves if we don't, indeed, love ourselves? How can we offer ourselves wholly and completely to the one who is worthy if we don't feel good about ourselves as an offering?

As you worship your Creator, it is time to align your sense of self-worth—how you see yourself—with what He says about you, with the worth He has ascribed to you! After all, you were made in the image of God—that alone gives you worth!

> Then God said, "Let us make human beings in our image, to be like us. They will reign over the fish in the sea, the birds in the sky, the livestock, all the wild animals on the earth, and the small animals that scurry along the ground." So God created human beings in his own image. In the image of God he created them; male and female he created them.
>
> **Genesis 1:26-27**

You—yes you—were fearfully and wonderfully made. He knit you together masterfully in your mother's womb. When is the last time you thanked God for making you the wonderful you that you are? How often do you praise Him as the master craftsman who not only created the vast and marvelous world we live in—but created you? David knew it and declared it! In the passage that began this chapter, he continued:

You watched me as I was being formed in utter seclusion,
　　as I was woven together in the dark of the womb.
You saw me before I was born.
　　Every day of my life was recorded in your book.
Every moment was laid out
　　before a single day had passed.

Psalm 139:15-16

Every feature of your body and personality is perfect to Him—don't argue! Every day and moment of your life matters. You are His own dear child: "But to all who believed him and accepted him, he gave the right to become children of God" (John 1:12) He challenges us to be our best, to pursue His holiness because we are special members of His family: "Imitate God, therefore, in everything you do, because you are his dear children" (Ephesians 5:1).

God knew you before you were born and dedicated you to do wonderful things. "I knew you before I formed you in your mother's womb. Before you were born I set you apart and appointed you as my prophet to the nations" (Jeremiah 1:5).

God has crowned you with honor.

When I look at the night sky and see the work of your
　　fingers—
　　the moon and the stars you set in place—
what are mere mortals that you should think about them,
　　human beings that you should care for them?
Yet you made them only a little lower than God
　　and crowned them with glory and honor.

Psalm 8:3-5

God knows every detail of your life and cares deeply for you.

What is the price of two sparrows—one copper coin? But not a single sparrow can fall to the ground without your Father knowing it. And the very hairs on your head are all numbered. So don't be afraid; you are more valuable to God than a whole flock of sparrows.

Matthew 10:29-31

You are precious to God. "Others were given in exchange for you. I traded their lives for yours because you are precious to me. You are honored, and I love you" (Isaiah 43:4).

You are God's child—you are a member of His family. "See how very much our Father loves us, for he calls us his children, and that is what we are!" (1 John 3:1).

God believes in you and has given you a purpose in life.

God decided in advance to adopt us into his own family by bringing us to himself through Jesus Christ. This is what he wanted to do, and it gave him great pleasure. So we praise God for the glorious grace he has poured out on us who belong to his dear Son.

Ephesians 1:5-6

For we are God's masterpiece. He has created us anew in Christ Jesus, so we can do the good things he planned for us long ago.

Ephesians 2:10

You are beautiful and without flaw. "You are altogether beautiful, my darling, beautiful in every way" (Song of Solomon 4:7).

Your true value is not skin-deep, but resides deep in your spirit.

Don't be concerned about the outward beauty of fancy hairstyles, expensive jewelry, or beautiful clothes. You should clothe yourselves instead with the beauty that comes from within, the unfading beauty of a gentle and quiet spirit, which is so precious to God.

1 Peter 3:3-4

If self-worth is a problem for you, go back and read the verses I just highlighted again. And again. Hear His words and truth about you and drink them in. Believe them. Embrace them in your heart and mind until there is no more argument. Worship Him by agreeing with Him!

Abraham Lincoln was president of the United States of America during the Civil War. His entire presidency was filled with intense bloodshed and strife. Even as he delivered his most famous speech, "The Emancipation Proclamation," freeing all slaves, I'm sure he was plagued with self-doubt at the cost of freedom. His critics were vicious. But he stayed true to his God-given course because he agreed with God. An earlier comment he made on self-worth is so instructive: "It is difficult to make a man miserable while he feels worthy of himself and claims kindred to the great God who made him."[1]

WHAT OTHERS SAY

You don't understand, Darlene.

She left me.

My father said I was no good.

I was turned down for a job because I was told I don't have what it takes.

I didn't do well in school—my teachers thought I was stupid.

No one finds me beautiful—no one gives me a second glance.

I'm not smart enough. I'm not good-looking enough. I'm not tall enough. I'm not thin enough. I don't speak well enough. I don't do anything right.

Whether delivered innocently or with malice, all of us have received messages that lower our sense of self-worth. Now, there are times when we should receive constructive correction as wisdom in order to grow fully into our best. Maybe we have a rough edge that grates on others' nerves. Maybe we need to give some thought to our appearance in order to look our best. But when words cut into our sense of being loved and valued by God at the level of our personhood, we must reject the message and agree with God: *I am wonderfully made just as I am; I am God's beloved; I am so precious to God that He sent Jesus Christ to die for my sins; I am beautiful in God's sight; I matter; I have a purpose.*

Can you say these words? Will you say them out loud right now—with full belief and confidence that they are true? Will you agree with God on how you look at yourself and what you see?

Your value is not based on the words of others. Negative voices, negative judgments, and criticisms will always be the loudest words we hear. This is human nature. That is why it is so imperative we listen to God's voice as we read His Word, as we pray, as we worship Him in His majesty.

That is one of the reasons David begins the Psalms by telling us we will be happy when we listen to Him and ignore the naysayers:

> Oh, the joys of those who do not
> > follow the advice of the wicked,
> > or stand around with sinners,
> > or join in with mockers.
> But they delight in the law of the Lord,
> > meditating on it day and night.
> They are like trees planted along the riverbank,
> > bearing fruit each season.
> Their leaves never wither, and they prosper in all they do.

Psalm 1:1-3

Words can bite and tear into us deeper than the teeth of a wild animal. Jesus reminds us that the Good Shepherd—and He is a Good Shepherd—builds up; false teachers and voices tear down:

> Those who heard Jesus use this illustration didn't understand what he meant, so he explained it to them: "I tell you the truth, I am the gate for the sheep. All who came before me were thieves and robbers. But the true sheep did not listen to them. Yes, I am the gate. Those who come in through me will

be saved. They will come and go freely and will find good pastures. The thief's purpose is to steal and kill and destroy. My purpose is to give them a rich and satisfying life."

John 10:6-10

Be a true sheep, obedient to the Good Shepherd. Listen to His voice, His words. When those who would rob you of abundant life, which includes your sense of self-worth and eternal value, come along, close your ears and heart.

I will say it again, though it sounds harsh. There are some people we simply can't fellowship with if we have the choice. Scoffers, criticizers, those who tear us down—they don't bring life because they don't speak the truth.

Victoria Osteen talks about how we find value in others, letting them determine how we feel about ourselves. Instead, we need to rest in the knowledge that we're children of God. She puts it this way:

> We should know that we are important because God says we are important. The value God placed on you is permanent. Nothing you can do, nothing anyone else can do, will ever be able to change that.[2]

To that I say amen—it is true!

WHEN YOU KNOW YOU ARE LOVED

When you know you are loved, there is a whole new level of living available to you. You can now love others because you love yourself. "Love your neighbor as yourself" (Mark 12:31). Until you love yourself, how can you truly love others in the way God intends you to?

You can worship boldly, knowing He invites you—yes, you—into His presence. "So let us come boldly to the throne of our gracious God. There we will receive his mercy, and we will find grace to help us when we need it most" (Hebrews 4:16).

You can confidently accomplish whatever task and destiny He has for you. "For I can do everything through Christ, who gives me strength" (Philippians 4:13). God desires proper humility, but not a lack of bold confidence.

You can walk through life free from the burdens of guilt and shame that accrue in life. You can get rid of the baggage that weighs you down, free from negative feelings that inhibit your effectiveness in building God's kingdom.

When Satan, the master liar and accuser, comes to rob you of the joy you have in your identity in Christ, you are able to declare with Paul:

> If God is for us, who can ever be against us? Since he did not spare even his own Son but gave him up for us all, won't he also give us everything else? Who dares accuse us whom God has chosen for his own? No one—for God himself has given us right standing with himself. Who then will condemn us? No one—for Christ Jesus died for us and was raised to life for us, and he is sitting in the place of honor at God's right hand, pleading for us.
>
> Can anything ever separate us from Christ's love? Does it mean he no longer loves us if we have trouble or calamity, or are persecuted, or hungry, or destitute, or in danger, or threatened with death? (As the Scriptures say, "For your sake we are killed every day; we are being slaughtered like sheep.") No, despite all these things, overwhelming victory is ours through Christ, who loved us.
>
> And I am convinced that nothing can ever separate us from God's love. Neither death nor life, neither angels nor demons, neither our fears for today nor our worries about tomorrow—not even the powers of hell can separate us from God's love. No power in the sky above or in the earth below—indeed, nothing in all creation will ever be able to separate us from the love of God that is revealed in Christ Jesus our Lord.
>
> Romans 8:31-39

I have found such hope and strength when I personalize God's Word by putting my name in the Scripture I am reading. The most important thing you might do in response to my encouragement about who you are in Christ is to do the same. *If God is for Darlene, who dares accuse Darlene? Nothing can separate Darlene from God's love, neither angels nor demons. Overwhelming victory is Darlene's through Christ who loves me.*

Put yourself in Scripture. Personalize it. Fill in your name. Let God's words and thoughts wash over you and inside of you.

You are God's beloved. He made you exactly the way you are for a reason. As Brennan Manning so eloquently prayed,

> Lord, when I feel that what I'm doing is insignificant and unimportant, help me to remember that everything I do is significant and important in your eyes, because you love me and you put me here, and no one else can do what I am doing in exactly the way I do it.[3]

When you know your identity in Christ—your priceless-ness—a whole new life awaits you. You will be strengthened to resist temptation—as well as the people who would use you for their own selfish desires rather than God's desires for you—as you walk in purity. "Don't you realize that all of you together are the temple of God and that the Spirit of God lives in you?" (1 Corinthians 3:16).

By God's grace, you will be able to turn perceived weaknesses into victories. Those things that the world calls a handicap, you can declare as a means for God's strength to reveal your true worth.

When you feel good about yourself, you will discover that correction and repentance become a way of life. I believe when we know how loved we are by God, we are much more able to receive constructive criticism—and know that it is different from destructive criticism. And not just from others but from God himself. John Ortberg Jr. put it this way:

Low self-esteem causes me to believe that I have so little worth that my response does not matter. With repentance, however, I understand that being worth so much to God is why my response is so important. Repentance is remedial work to mend our minds and hearts, which get bent by sin.[4]

Paul was brilliant and driven. It doesn't seem possible that he would lack for confidence. Yet the Roman historian Josephus referred disparagingly to his physical appearance by calling him "the ugly Jew." That didn't slow Paul down one bit from his God-given destiny. Not even a physical handicap could knock him off his stride—though it was a matter of prayer for him:

> Three different times I begged the Lord to take it away. Each time he said, "My grace is all you need. My power works best in weakness." So now I am glad to boast about my weaknesses, so that the power of Christ can work through me. That's why I take pleasure in my weaknesses, and in the insults, hardships, persecutions, and troubles that I suffer for Christ. For when I am weak, then I am strong.
>
> 2 Corinthians 12:8-10

Isn't that just like Paul? The very thing in his life that could rob him of his sense of worth and value became something he bragged about! Now that's confidence. That's knowing who you are in Christ.

THE TREASURE INSIDE YOU

Yes, some of us have been wounded. We carry scars. We have done things that damaged us—and others have damaged us as well. Never lose heart. Never believe you are worthless. Our worth—the treasure we have—is inside us: "We now have this light shining in our hearts, but we ourselves are like fragile clay jars containing this great treasure. This makes it clear that our great power is from God, not from ourselves" (2 Corinthians 4:7).

If you took a one hundred dollar bill out of your pocket and dropped it on the ground and it got wet and a little muddy, would you throw it away? Would you say it is no longer worth anything? Of course not. The bill is still worth one hundred dollars. You would pick it up and spend it at its full value.

Some things get damaged in life and are worthless. If your car gets a dent in its side, its value decreases. If you rip a piece of artwork, it won't command the same price at auction. If you own a beautiful stretch of land with majestic hardwoods that are destroyed by a forest fire, the property value might go down. But even with hurts and scars from the wear and tear of life, you won't lose value. Your value is based on God's declaration of who you are. Wrinkles, a few dents, and a few setbacks won't diminish you.

In fact, not even the dark stain of sin can subtract from your worth. Even sin reveals your worth because of the price God paid for it:

> For you know that God paid a ransom to save you from the empty life you inherited from your ancestors. And it was not paid with mere gold or silver, which lose their value. It was the precious blood of Christ, the sinless, spotless Lamb of God. God chose him as your ransom long before the world began, but now in these last days he has been revealed for your sake.
>
> 1 Peter 1:18-20

David, a hero of faith, knew the internal agony of sinning greatly against God and man. But his deep understanding of God's faithful love allowed him to proclaim, "Purify me from my sins, and I will be clean; wash me, and I will be whiter than snow" (Psalm 51:7).

Hallelujah! That is something to praise God for. He is so good. Worship Him with all your heart and all your life. Worship Him for all you are *worth*—because you are worth so much to Him!

CHAPTER 15

MY WORK

*Work willingly at whatever you do, as though
you were working for the Lord rather than for people.
Remember that the Lord will give you
an inheritance as your reward, and that
the Master you are serving is Christ.*

COLOSSIANS 3:23-24

WORSHIP GOD THROUGH OUR WORK? *Really? C'mon, Darlene. Work is hard and stressful. It's busy. It's not a place I feel very spiritual. I'm so glad when work is over. I can relax. And if I'm not too tired, I have some time with God. I don't see how I can worship God at work—it seems to be the place that most keeps me away from Him.*

Have you ever thought or said something similar to that sentiment?

Many of us spend more waking hours with our work colleagues than with our families—it may be where we spend more time than anywhere else but home. If God is present everywhere—and we know He is—and if worship is spending time in His presence, acknowledging and glorifying Him, then we need to wake up and simply keep Jesus at the center in *all* things, even our workplace.

Some need to heed the simple advice of Billy Graham: "Read the Bible. Work hard and honestly. Don't complain."[1] I like that! Or how about Zig Ziglar telling us, "A lot of people quit looking for work as soon as they find a job!"[2] These are good reminders to work hard, but if we take the words of Paul seriously, we discover that when we work heartily, as *for the Lord* and not for man, work becomes an act of worship.

I know that we all want to find personal enrichment and fulfillment in our careers, and that doesn't seem possible in all jobs. But ultimately, when we work as to our Lord, every task, great or small, becomes an offering of praise to the one who gives us the reward that matters most in life: His favor.

So as we start, let's shrug off popular but erroneous thinking about work, namely that it is a necessary evil. Yes, work became harder through the fall:

> "The ground is cursed because of you. All your life you will struggle to scratch a living from it. It will grow thorns and thistles for you, though you will eat of its grains. By the sweat of your brow will you have food to eat until you return to the ground from which you were made."
>
> Genesis 3:17-19

But don't miss two obvious truths. First, God gave Adam work to do *before* the fall:

> The Lord God placed the man in the Garden of Eden to tend and watch over it. . . . So the Lord God formed from the ground all the wild animals and all the birds of the sky. He brought them to the man to see what he would call them, and the man chose a name for each one. He gave names to all the livestock, all the birds of the sky, and all the wild animals.
>
> Genesis 2:15, 19-20

Second, the second Adam, our Lord and Savior Jesus Christ, is redeeming all things through His death and resurrection, including work:

> For [even the whole] creation (all nature) waits expectantly and longs earnestly for God's sons to be made known [waits for the revealing, the disclosing of their sonship]. For the

creation (nature) was subjected to frailty (to futility, condemned to frustration), not because of some intentional fault on its part, but by the will of Him Who so subjected it—[yet] with the hope that nature (creation) itself will be set free from its bondage to decay and corruption [and gain an entrance] into the glorious freedom of God's children.

Romans 8:19-21 AMPLIFIED

Paul's advice on work was, "Make it your goal to live a quiet life, minding your own business and working with your hands" (1 Thessalonians 4:11). We've talked about how being positive in our attitudes is an act of worship. Let's be positive about our work. Thank God for the opportunity to earn a wage and serve Him and others through our labors.

WHAT YOU GONNA DO WITH WHAT YOU GOT?

Jesus tells us a fascinating story of three servants that has multiple applications. In the parable of the talents, a master gives three of his employees a sum of money to put to work while he is away on a business trip. What will they do with no one to supervise them?

One gets five talents, the second two talents, and the third one talent. The first two servants invest the money and are able to offer the boss a tidy profit upon his return. Both are suitably rewarded. The third does nothing other than bury the money in his backyard. When the boss returns, he sheepishly gives back what he got. The judgment is sharp and rough:

"You wicked and lazy servant, you knew that I reap where I have not sown, and gather where I have not scattered seed. So you ought to have deposited my money with the bankers, and at my coming I would have received back my own with interest. Therefore take the talent from him, and give it to him who has ten talents."

Matthew 25:26-28 NKJV

The parable teaches us the principle that we are to use the gifts God has given us, both spiritually and in the world of commerce. The question this parable raises is simple and profound: What are you going to do with what you have? What are you going to do with the work in your life? You might have a ten-talent or five-talent or one-talent job, but God expects you to be faithful, to give your best in all you do as service as worship to Him.

I believe it is okay to want more, to have a healthy ambition at work and not be satisfied with our current roles. But don't forget that greater responsibility and rewards come when we are faithful with what we've been given right now. It's okay to feel dissatisfaction with having only one talent, but don't let that become a negativity that poisons your attitudes—and the attitudes of others—at work. Work as unto the Lord, remembering that He is the one who promotes you. I believe our King James Version puts this so clearly and powerfully, and I believe the message literally: "For promotion cometh neither from the east, nor from the west, nor from the south. But God is the judge: he putteth down one, and setteth up another" (Psalm 75:6-7).

But never forget that the ultimate reward for your work is from God himself. Paul counsels the baby church in Colossae: "Work willingly at whatever you do, as though you were working for the Lord rather than for people. Remember that the Lord will give you an inheritance as your reward, and that the Master you are serving is Christ" (Colossians 3:23-24).

If you are cleaning floors, make sure your Lord has the cleanest floors to walk on. If you are serving coffee, make sure your Lord receives His cup just the way he ordered it and with a warm smile. If you are an accountant, make sure the financial books are done so well that God would be proud to show them to an auditor. If you are a nurse, make sure that your Lord receives your very best tender loving care. If you repair automobiles, make sure the Lord's means of transportation are safe and right. If you are a stay-at-home mom, raise your children with the Word of God as your anchor, bringing glory to Him. If you feel stuck in a dead-end job, make sure you work to the admiring eye of God himself—and trust Him for promotion. If you are running a billion-dollar enterprise, do all you can to succeed with integrity as a witness and so you are able to bless others through honorable and fair employment.

The nineteenth-century American minister Henry Ward Beecher, who was an ardent and compassionate champion to free the slaves (and whose sister Harriet Beecher Stowe wrote the classic *Uncle Tom's Cabin*) offered this gem of wisdom:

> When God wanted sponges and oysters He made them and put one on a rock and the other in the mud. When He made man, He did not make him to be a sponge or an oyster; He made him with feet and hands, and head and heart, and vital blood, and a place to use them and He said to him, "Go! Work!"[3]

WORK AS AN OBEDIENT WITNESS

In Acts 1, the risen Christ gives His disciples a mighty task: "Be my witnesses, telling people about me everywhere—in Jerusalem, throughout Judea, in Samaria, and to the ends of the earth" (Acts 1:8). He also gives one very specific instruction to Peter and the others: "Do not leave Jerusalem until the Father sends you the gift he promised, as I told you before. John baptized with water, but in just a few days you will be baptized with the Holy Spirit" (vv. 4-5). What did Jesus tell Peter to do? Nothing. Don't act in the flesh—wait for the Spirit. What is the first thing Peter does? He acts in the flesh. He says, "We need a twelfth disciple" (see v. 21). Had he received the Spirit yet? No. He did things his way. The result was the first argument in the brand-new baby church—some wanted Matthias, others wanted Barsabbas (vv. 23-26).

You would think our first church leader would have realized by now to listen to his Lord and stop, to not make a bad matter worse. But he didn't listen. Peter pressed on and made the decision about who would be the new apostle by throwing dice. In his mind, this wasn't gambling; it was letting God decide. After all, there are numerous instances in the Old Testament when determining God's will was done by the casting of lots. But that practice was part of the ceremonial religion that was replaced by the New Testament—the New Covenant. Peter ignored Jesus' instructions, and when he got in a bind with a church argument, he reverted to his former religious life.

As you read through the New Testament, it is quite clear that Matthias was not God's choice for apostle. I'm sure he was a good man, but he wasn't anointed for that position. His name was never mentioned in Scripture again.

Jesus himself called the twelfth apostle: Saul of Tarsus. But Peter's decision to act outside of the Spirit meant that Paul (Greek for Saul), would continuously have to defend his apostleship. That's why he often begins his letters like he did in Galatians, where he said, "This letter is from Paul, an apostle. I was not appointed by any group of people or any human authority, but by Jesus Christ himself and by God the Father, who raised Jesus from the dead" (Galatians 1:1).

Paul was faithful to his anointing. He was a fiercely intelligent man of great integrity. In defending himself he was embarrassed to brag about his credentials. But he never apologized for one personal defense he gave to support his right to preach the gospel of Christ. That defense was his work ethic:

> You know that these hands of mine have worked to supply my own needs and even the needs of those who were with me. And I have been a constant example of how you can help those in need by working hard.
>
> Acts 20:34-35

This great theologian, missionary, writer, and apostle—called by Jesus himself—was proud to be a tentmaker in order to prove he was preaching not for personal gain but for the approval of his God. After a long day of preaching, witnessing, and visiting, he pulled out the tools of his trade and created tents for and to the glory of God.

Whether in an office, on the factory floor, on top of a roof with hammer and nails, or in the pulpit bringing forth God's Word, your work is a testimony. Does your work obediently tell others what you feel about God? Do you honor His name?

Jesus was a carpenter. He learned at His earthly father's knee. Is it any wonder He saw such potential in everyday workers—from fishermen to tax collectors to soldiers?

IS IT POSSIBLE TO WORK TOO MUCH?

Do some people spend too much time at work and put it on a pedestal as a false idol? In his book *The Rhythm of Life*,[4] Richard Exley says that for life to be whole we need four things: rest, play, work, worship.

Undoubtedly we can let life get out of balance and rhythm. While going through treatment for cancer, I learned that I had too often ignored rest. In that season I had no choice but to honor God's principle of the Sabbath—man's need for rest.

Work is to be worship—but we can't worship work. If your self-worth and your sense of importance is too tightly aligned to your work, remember that you are doing it for the Lord to regain a proper perspective. For farmers there are seasons when the hours of toil will begin early and end late or else they will lose their harvest. So the nature of one's work must be considered when determining how much work is enough. But don't farmers have a few months each year that are less labor intensive? Some of us will have to purposely create a down season when our batteries can be recharged and there is more time to spend with loved ones in laughter and play.

My caution is not against hard work—but to keep life in balance. I personally love to use the words "God-ordained daily purpose." Sometimes the word *balance* causes us to respond by putting life in boxes, but I just pray for the Holy Spirit to lead and direct. Work, rest, and play, woven in and out of each other.

Two giants of the faith had keen insights on keeping work within the total rhythm of life. Martin Luther said: "Tomorrow I plan to work, work, from early until late. In fact I have so much to do that I shall spend the first three hours in prayer."[5] John Wesley said, "Though I am always in a haste, I am never in a hurry, because I never undertake more work than I can go through with perfect calmness of spirit."[6] How inspiring.

RELATIONSHIPS AT WORK

One of the most amazing books in the Bible is only one short chapter long, written by Paul to a man named Philemon. Philemon was a slave owner. One of his slaves, Onesimus, had run away, and while on the run he became a follower of Jesus and a co-worker with Paul. Slavery was a standard practice of the day. It wasn't always a lifelong status, and it often took the form of a contract with a set number of years of service. But we still know that being a slave was demeaning and against God's plan for mankind.

Onesimus did not want to be looking over his shoulder the rest of his life, and he and Paul determined it was best that he return to Philemon—also a believer—and set things right. Wow. What an act of courage and obedience. Though Paul did not specifically prohibit slavery in his letters, his counsel to masters to not be harsh and his words to Philemon were a huge driving force in ending this heinous practice that is sadly still alive in parts of the world today. Paul's appeal to Philemon is winsome and brilliant—how can this follower of Christ turn Paul down?

> I have a favor to ask of you. As Christ's ambassador and now a prisoner for him, I wouldn't hesitate to command this if I thought it necessary, but I'd rather make it a personal request.
> While here in jail, I've fathered a child, so to speak. And here he is, hand-carrying this letter—Onesimus! He was useless to you before; now he's useful to both of us. I'm sending him back to you, but it feels like I'm cutting off my right arm

in doing so. I wanted in the worst way to keep him here as your stand-in to help out while I'm in jail for the Message. But I didn't want to do anything behind your back, make you do a good deed that you hadn't willingly agreed to.

Maybe it's all for the best that you lost him for a while. You're getting him back now for good—and no mere slave this time, but a true Christian brother! That's what he was to me—he'll be even more than that to you.

So if you still consider me a comrade-in-arms, welcome him back as you would me. If he damaged anything or owes you anything, chalk it up to my account. This is my personal signature—Paul—and I stand behind it. (I don't need to remind you, do I, that you owe your very life to me?) Do me this big favor, friend. You'll be doing it for Christ, but it will also do my heart good. I know you well enough to know you will. You'll probably go far beyond what I've written.

Philemon 1:8-21 THE MESSAGE

Though the thought of slavery in any form is rightfully repugnant, Paul's words were revolutionary at the time he wrote them. Consider a slave as a brother?! He was sounding the death knell for the false barriers of a "class system" between people, including between bosses and employers. Can you imagine the shockwaves throughout the Roman Empire when he wrote about relationships in the church, "There is no longer Jew or Gentile, slave or free, male and female" (Galatians 3:28)?

The workplace is one of those unique opportunities to show how God sees each and every person on the face of the earth as equal in value and worth. Whether you're a leader or a follower, at the top or at the bottom, work becomes a place to express proper pride, humility, and respect. It becomes a place of worship! Francis de Sales, a seventeenth-century mystic, said, "We must never undervalue any person. The workman loves not that his work should be despised in his presence. Now God is present everywhere, and every person is His work."[7]

When you see injustice and mistreatment in the workplace, take the words of Paul to heart:

> The world is unprincipled. It's dog-eat-dog out there! The world doesn't fight fair. But we don't live or fight our battles that way—never have and never will. The tools of our trade aren't for marketing or manipulation, but they are for demolishing that entire massively corrupt culture. We use our powerful God-tools for smashing warped philosophies, tearing down barriers erected against the truth of God, fitting every loose thought and emotion and impulse into the structure of life shaped by Christ. Our tools are ready at hand for clearing the ground of every obstruction and building lives of obedience into maturity.
>
> 2 Corinthians 10:3-6 THE MESSAGE

Work is such a wonderful place to build relationships of mutual respect that will introduce the good news of God's love. Tyrants become merciful. Rebels become respectful. God's love is poured out when even one person (maybe you, and maybe this is why you work where you do) brings love and respect to all of his or her co-workers.

LET GOD HELP!

If work is worship, what does it mean when you don't know what to do? As part of your worship, go to God for help, of course!

Dietrich Bonhoeffer said this about the demands of work:

> Temptations which accompany the working day will be conquered on the basis of the morning breakthrough to God. Decisions, demanded by work, become easier and simpler where they are made not in the fear of men, but only in the sight of God. . . . He wants to give us today the power which we need for our work.[8]

James puts it this way: "If you need wisdom, ask our generous God, and he will give it to you" (James 1:5).

Have you asked God to help you in your work recently? Have you praised God for your work? Have you said thanks to Him? The words of Thomas Carlyle offer a great perspective: "Blessed is he who has found his work; let him ask no other blessedness. He has a work, a life-purpose; he has found it, and will follow it! . . . Labor is life."[9]

There's so much to think about in the area of work and worship. There are few areas of life more misunderstood from a spiritual perspective. If work is an area of defeat for you, ask God for help. Begin your work with the simple statement, "By your grace I see this work as worship." See what difference that statement alone makes! "By your grace, O Lord, *I am doing this with you*." This is your spiritual worship—and worship changes everything.

I want to remind you that God gives you all the strength you need for the tasks in front of you with this quote from Elisabeth Elliot:

> Work is a blessing. God has so arranged the world that work is necessary, and He gives us hands and strength to do it. The enjoyment of leisure would be nothing if we had only leisure. It is the joy of work well done that enables us to enjoy rest, just as it is the experiences of hunger and thirst that make food and drink such pleasures.[10]

I worship you in all that I do, my Lord and Savior. I worship you in my work.

CHAPTER 16

OUR MARRIAGE

"For this reason a man will leave his father and mother
and be united to his wife, and the two will become one flesh."
So they are no longer two, but one flesh.
Therefore what God has joined together, let no one separate.

MARK 10:7–9 NIV

BEFORE GOD CALLED ABRAHAM, before He made a covenant with His chosen people, before He delivered His children from slavery, before He gave the law, before He sent His only begotten Son to save the world from its sins, before He sent the Holy Spirit on the day of Pentecost to birth the church, before all that, God created marriage.

He created Adam and Eve and gave them to each other as a blessing and a gift. He sealed the relationship with His presence. That is why the wedding ceremony is an act of worship—but not just the ceremony, the entire relationship. God himself was the minister at the world's first wedding.

> So the Lord God caused the man to fall into a deep sleep. While the man slept, the Lord God took out one of the man's ribs and closed up the opening. Then the Lord God made a woman from the rib, and he brought her to the man.
>
> "At last!" the man exclaimed. "This one is bone from my bone, and flesh from my flesh! She will be called 'woman,' because she was taken from 'man.'"

> This explains why a man leaves his father and mother and
> is joined to his wife, and the two are united into one.
>
> Genesis 2:21-24

Max Lucado, such a gifted communicator, puts marriage in this spiritual perspective: "God created marriage. No government subcommittee envisioned it. No social organization developed it. Marriage was conceived and born in the mind of God."[1]

Because God has ordained marriage, it is holy ground. At the same time, you honor your spouse, you honor your children, and you become a bold witness of God's plan for man and woman. I want to explore some aspects of the central dynamics of love and honor that make a wonderful marriage even more wonderful, that restore a struggling marriage, and that deepen your spiritual walk with the Lord.

Let me say to those who are single and reading this book, you may think this chapter doesn't apply to you. I would still encourage you to read on. I believe there are vital worship insights to be found in God's plan for marriage.

A DELIGHTFUL STATE OF LOVE

Marriage is a holy, pleasing relationship that is God-ordained. It may be under fire by teachings that are abundant in the world today, but it is still precious to the heart of God.

When God created the heavens and the earth and everything in it, He looked at what He had done and said, "This is very good" (see Genesis 31:1). When Adam saw Eve, I suspect he echoed God's delight in His creation and said, "Yes, this is *very* good!" When God gave Adam and Eve to each other as man and wife, He was giving the gifts of companionship, comfort, help, delight, and love to each of them.

To anyone who doubts that God created marriage to be a true delight, I would direct them to the Song of Solomon. Yes, Solomon's words can teach us *allegorically* about God's love and delight in His people, but the book is also *literally* what it is: the story and description of a man and a woman so in love, so attracted, so passionate for one another they can barely contain their joy—and can't keep their hands off each other! But don't take my word for it. Read it yourself. This is God's idea!

Solomon's words are groundbreaking. He is putting love and commitment and passion into a relationship that was far too often nothing more than a legal agreement based on an exchange of goods or even international diplomacy.

The young man in the story says to his beloved: "How beautiful you are, my darling, how beautiful! Your eyes are like doves" (Song of Solomon 1:15). Her reply is quite saucy: "You are so handsome, my love, pleasing beyond words! The soft grass is our bed; fragrant cedar branches are the beams of our house, and pleasant smelling firs are the rafters" (vv. 16-17). Those few verses just might tempt you to read more about the delight of a lover and his beloved.

No marriage will live in a perpetual state of bliss and romance. We work. We raise kids. We pay bills. We fix broken appliances and patch leaky roofs. But we do these things together as a team. Even when we argue, we are on the same side, united in love for each other and God. When Mark and I had been married twenty years, my Nan, who graduated to heaven at the ripe old age of 100 (I have attended three of my grandparents' hundredth birthday parties!), sent us a card that said, "Congratulations! The first twenty are the worst!" She and Pop were married seventy-seven years before he passed away at 101 years old. She explained her comment by saying that the first twenty years are filled with little money, having children, buying a home, etc. A lot of pressure. But she said to me that so many don't hang around for the really *rich* years! She was *such* an inspiration to me and many others.

One of the ways God asks us to show love for Him is through how we love our spouse and treat our marriage bonds. In a world of brokenness, what a marvelous way to worship God. This is no drudgery. What joy you will find as you love God in your active, passionate, determined, faithful, joyful love of your spouse.

If you feel you have fallen out of love with your spouse—if marriage isn't a delight for you right now—remember that love is a *verb*, not a *noun*. In his book *Mere Christianity*, C. S. Lewis reminds us:

> Love as distinct from "being in love" is not merely a feeling. It is a deep unity, maintained by the will and deliberately strengthened by habit; reinforced by (in Christian marriages) the grace which both partners ask, and receive from God. They can have this love for each other even at those moments when they do not like each other; as you love yourself even when you do not like yourself.[2]

Love is active. Don't worry yourself about the state of your emotions in a day or season of life. Get busy loving. The apostle Paul gives a great way to show love to your spouse:

> Love is patient and kind. Love is not jealous or boastful or proud or rude. It does not demand its own way. It is not irritable, and it keeps no record of being wronged. It does not rejoice about injustice but rejoices whenever the truth wins out. Love never gives up, never loses faith, is always hopeful, and endures through every circumstance.

> **1 Corinthians 13:4-7**

Worship is about loving God and, through His love, loving others. Worship is an act of obedience. Worship is a decision that calls for us to exercise our will. No matter how glum things look right now, don't believe the lies of Satan that your marriage cannot be saved and become all God wants it to be. If you are surrounded by people who don't honor marriage—and specifically *your* marriage—surround yourself with a new group of people. Don't lose heart and give up. Ask the Holy Spirit to give you the grace you need on the journey. If you believe your marriage is worth fighting for, you'll do whatever it takes as far as is in your power to do so.

Listen to the wise counsel of Timothy Keller in his book *The Meaning of Marriage*:

> In any relationship, there will be frightening spells in which your feelings of love dry up. And when that happens you must remember that the essence of marriage is that it is a covenant, a commitment, a promise of future love. So what do you do? You do the acts of love, despite your lack of feeling. You may not feel tender, sympathetic, and eager to please, but in your actions you must be tender, understanding, forgiving and helpful. And, if you do that, as time goes on you will not only get through the dry spells, but they will become less frequent and deep, and you will become more constant in your feelings. This is what can happen if you decide to love.[3]

Choose God's way. Decide. Act. Be willing to show love as your worship to God. Our God is so good at creating love; let Him take care of the rest. He will restore the passion and tender feelings that might be missing in this season of life.

LOVE AND RESPECT

In Ephesians 5:21, Paul sets up his famous passage on marriage with a simple principle: "Submit to one another out of reverence for Christ." Do you see how close the connection is between marriage and worship? *Submitting to one another* uses the same wording as when we submit to God in worship. It is a declaration of surrender and honor. *The two shall become one.* How you care for, submit to, and honor your spouse is how you care for yourself—and God.

As we continue to read Ephesians 5, Paul says that wives are to "submit to your husbands as to the Lord" (v. 22). Husbands are to "love your wives, just as Christ loved the church" (v. 25). Those are powerful words, filled with commitment and responsibility and trust—and joy.

I love speaking heart to heart with women, but it breaks my heart that so many women feel unloved. They feel none of the beauty that Solomon describes of his beloved. Paul's words to "submit to your husbands" are a struggle. Submitting doesn't feel fair, reasonable, or safe. They haven't seen the love of Christ from their husbands and don't want to submit.

In the same way, there are countless men who don't feel they are treated in a way that makes it easy to love their wives. They don't feel loved either. I believe one of the best contemporary marriage books is *Love and Respect*, written by Emerson Eggerichs. He describes the transformational miracle that happens in a marriage when these verses are applied by men and women:

> We believe love best motivates a woman and respect most powerfully motivates a man. Research reveals that during marital conflict a husband most often reacts when feeling disrespected and a wife reacts when feeling unloved. . . . Though we all need love and respect equally, the felt-need differs during conflict, and this difference is as different as pink is from blue![4]

In the story of Esther, the queen who saved her people by risking her own life. Her husband was not a follower of God. He governed ruthlessly. But her sense of destiny—*you were born for such a time as this*—spilled over in obedience. The way she moved the heart of the king, the man who had given the order to have her people killed, was by honoring him—not because he was acting honorably, but because she was honoring her God.

> On the third day of the fast, Esther put on her royal robes and entered the inner court of the palace, just across from the king's hall. The king was sitting on his royal throne, facing the entrance. When he saw Queen Esther standing there in the inner court, he welcomed her and held out the gold scepter to her. So Esther approached and touched the end of the scepter. Then the king asked her, "What do you want, Queen Esther?

What is your request? I will give it to you, even if it is half the kingdom!"

Esther 5:1-3

Love and respect—he, she, we need both. Worship gives God the glory. Honoring your marriage vows honors Him. I'll say it again: Don't be lulled to sleep by the spirit of the world that says marriage is a casual agreement that is good in the good times but disposable in the bad times. It truly is for better or worse.

John Piper, in a paraphrase of Paul's words in Ephesians 5:25-33, reminds us that when we don't honor marriage we actually dishonor ourselves:

> Husbands and wives, recognize that in marriage you have become one flesh. If you live for your private pleasure at the expense of your spouse, you are living against yourself and destroying your joy. But if you devote yourself with all your heart to the holy joy of your spouse, you will also be living for your joy and making a marriage after the image of Christ and his church.[5]

FAITHFULNESS

Marriage is a covenant that God establishes between a man and a woman for a lifetime. Faithfulness to your spouse shows faithfulness to God. So many marriages today are torn apart by infidelity. Men or women don't fall into the trap of affairs because they planned to fool around with others as they stood at the altar and gave their vows. You don't fall into these situations because you have no control. It happens on the slippery slope of compromise and poor decision-making; it happens because the flames of intimacy are not kindled and cared for; it happens because we lose the sense of how holy this relationship is. Marriage is a refuge, a sanctuary.

Guard this sanctuary. Don't let anyone else inside this bond of love and commitment. I believe there are clear boundaries we must establish between us and members of the opposite sex. I know some husbands and wives agree that they won't have meals with a member of the opposite sex without their spouse present or at minimum in a group setting.

If you are going through a spiritual struggle and need the counsel of a wise Christian, I would encourage you not to open your heart up to a member of the opposite sex. Don't build a bond of intimacy outside your marriage bonds. If you feel someone else is taking too keen an interest in you, set boundaries. Don't entertain the attention. We are to love all our brothers and sisters, but there is an exclusive intimacy that is between you and your spouse alone.

Jealousy is not a healthy emotion. It is often a sign of insecurity, not proof of an outside threat or proof of greater devotion. But if your spouse does feel jealous and has concerns about someone in particular, listen to him or her. They may see something you don't recognize. Honor them—even if their jealousy is based on insecurity.

Faithfulness is not just about the physical. Show fidelity through what you say about your spouse. Some people joke about their spouse, not intending to be disrespectful. But I don't believe that is wise. When we criticize and complain about our spouse publicly, we are not showing love and honor. Perhaps there is a private spiritual counseling session when negative things can be said. But even in a private setting with a trusted spiritual mentor, negativity should not be the focus of our thoughts and words about our spouse. We show fidelity by our words. The first command is to honor the name of God—to never take His name in vain.

Words. So small. So big. So powerful. What do your words to and about your spouse say? I believe many troubled marriages could be saved by taming the tongue.

If there has been infidelity in your marriage, know that all is not lost. As we discussed in the story of Hosea, God himself knows what it feels like to have His bride—His people—chase after other lovers. It broke His heart. It angered Him. But ultimately His love and His faithfulness would not let her go: "But then I will win her back once again. I will lead her into the desert and speak tenderly to her there" (Hosea 2:14).

Infidelity is so damaging and hurtful to all parties involved. But know that God's love is greater than any sin we commit. G. K. Chesterton said, "Charity means pardoning the unpardonable, or it is no virtue at all. Hope means hoping when things are hopeless, or it is no virtue at all. And faith means believing the incredible, or it is no virtue at all."[6] True repentance and true forgiveness can restore even the most hopeless of relationships. Reconcile if at all possible for your spouse, for yourself, but most of all, for God.

A young woman, six months pregnant, discovered her husband was having an affair. She then found out it wasn't his first or second or third fling. She was devastated. She was broken to the point of considering suicide.

A wise and wonderful Christian woman came to her rescue. "Honey, when I was young, I was taught that there are some situations so hard we have to just lay prostrate before God. Sometimes we need to pray and fast and get a group to join with us."

That dear young wife, so shattered, lay face-down before God. She gathered a group of women to pray and fast on a particular day for her marriage. Her husband had left the house and moved in with his latest girlfriend. But on the day she and her friends prayed and fasted, he was pierced in his heart. He felt the full measure of his sin. He came home with a penitent spirit. The marriage was saved.

I can't tell you that will happen that way for you, but I can promise you with every fiber of my being that you will find God is faithful—and He is, after all, the husband of the widow and the father of the fatherless.

Your faithfulness will be rewarded. Her faithfulness turned her husband's unfaithful heart back to God and home. Miracles do happen.

WORSHIP TOGETHER

Do you read Scripture and pray with your spouse?

We are too busy. We mean to, but then we get going in the day and it doesn't happen. We're just too busy.

If you are too busy to share time in worship with your spouse, you are too busy! I think morning is best—a time to focus on God and each other at the start of the day. If that's not possible, any time will do. This can be a short time or an extended period. The important thing is that your hearts are united in praise and worship together. Even if you are traveling, a moment of prayer *together* on the telephone can bring you together across the miles.

One of the keys to a successful marriage is to have a *shared common purpose*. It can be a business. It can be raising kids. It can be a ministry or outreach. Those are all great things. But the greatest common purpose is to worship and honor the one who is worthy of all praise. I fell in love with Mark when I knew He had an unrelenting pursuit of Christ that was greater than his love for me. Because once God had his heart, I knew I would always be safe. He was a man who followed after God and His purposes. Our marriage has been built around the cause of Christ. Has it been without challenges? No. Has it been without regrets? No. But God is good, and through His agape love shed abroad in our hearts, He makes all things new. Business and other projects will have a beginning and an end. But God has called us to worship Him for eternity—and that's long enough for any marriage!

Worship together!

REKINDLE INTIMACY

Don't forget the importance of intimacy. Sex was God's idea, and that makes it a very good thing. Intimacy brings out all the qualities that are part of worship: trust, delight, giving oneself fully to another, passion, and love. Don't neglect the marriage bed. In fact, I fully believe that a couple that shares the bonds of worship will share the most remarkable sex life.

There is a myth perpetuated by the world that Christians are against sex. I believe this fabrication is a lie of Satan to turn hearts against God through scorn and slander—and even make followers of Christ wonder if enjoying sex makes them less than spiritual.

I do believe that one of the reasons this slander is so persistent is that as Christians we do not accept casual sex, promiscuous sex, or sex without love and commitment.

C. S. Lewis put it this way:

> If anyone says that sex, in itself, is bad, Christianity contradicts him at once. But, of course, when people say, "Sex is nothing to be ashamed of," they may mean "the state into which the sexual instinct has now got is nothing to be ashamed of."
>
> If they mean that, I think they are wrong. I think it is everything to be ashamed of. There is nothing to be ashamed of in enjoying your food: there would be everything to be ashamed of if half the world made food the main interest of their lives and spent their time looking at pictures of food and dribbling and smacking their lips.[7]

Sex is a wonderful gift from God. It is a wonderful expression of love, trust, honor—and delight.

John MacArthur, a gifted Bible teacher, puts it quite strongly:

> Sexual expression within a marriage is not an option or an extra. It is certainly not, as it has sometimes been considered, a necessary evil in which spiritual Christians engage only to procreate children. It is far more than a physical act. God created it to be the expression and experience of love on the deepest human level and to be a beautiful and powerful bond between husband and wife.[8]

Worship God in your marriage, and experience His most precious and profound gift of delight in the marriage bed. A great piece of simple advice is this: As married couples, don't forgo making love together for too long. Long periods of no intimacy in a marriage can make a fairly simple life very, very complicated. Make the time and enjoy each other, for the joy of unity in a marriage brings security on so many levels.

START WHERE YOU ARE

If your marriage isn't a sanctuary, a place of spiritual worship, start where you are:

- Bring your marriage to God, lay it at His feet, and ask Him for His blessing and help.

- Confess where your marriage has fallen short—God knows everything already, so don't hold back. This is His way of asking you to be completely honest.

- Commit to love and honor your spouse, even if you are acting alone. Remember, even if you are not feeling particularly loving and respectful of your spouse at this moment, you are doing it for God.

- Pray for your marriage—and if at all possible, in your marriage. Do all you can to find common purpose in love for God.

- Speak words of life to your spouse and eliminate words that tear down and curse. Be disciplined and obedient in your testimony.

- Ask your spouse to forgive you, and forgive your spouse as God forgave you. Don't go to bed angry! Apologize quickly and sincerely. Make peace. Don't let small grievances grow into a mountain of resentment!

I'll say it again for emphasis: I hope and pray that you can do this as a *team*. But even if you must act alone for now, know that God's plans for you are for good and not for harm, to prosper you and keep your heart in perfect peace.

A NOTE TO THE SINGLE

Maybe you are single and have never married, whether you have a desire to be married or not. Maybe you are divorced or widowed. If that's the case, at this time in your life, let God be your spouse. Draw nearer to Him as He draws near to you. I'm not just writing to women, but to men as well. We all desire intimacy and the feeling of being loved, of being special. God meets us right where we are and will flood our hearts with His presence, so we know we are the beloved. Don't pursue an unhealthy relationship to feel loved. Pursue God.

Worship and honor God with your purity. There are so many voices out there telling us that casual intimacy is no big deal, and that no one gets hurt. There is such a bond between spirituality and sexuality that I just don't believe this is true. Paul teaches us:

> There's more to sex than mere skin on skin. Sex is as much spiritual mystery as physical fact. As written in Scripture, "The two become one." Since we want to become spiritually one with the Master, we must not pursue the kind of sex that avoids commitment and intimacy, leaving us more lonely than ever—the kind of sex that can never "become one." There is a sense in which sexual sins are different from all others. In sexual sin we violate the sacredness of our own bodies, these bodies that were made for God-given and God-modeled love, for "becoming one" with another. Or didn't you realize that your body is a sacred place, the place of the Holy Spirit? Don't you see that you can't live however you please, squandering what God paid such a high price for? The physical part of you is not some piece of property belonging to the spiritual part of you. God owns the whole works. So let people see God in and through your body.
>
> 1 Corinthians 6:18-20 The Message

Honoring God with your purity is worship. It will be the best way to prepare yourself for marriage, if that is to be. Before marrying again or for the first time, go back through the verses and thoughts in this chapter. Paul says, "Don't team up with those who are unbelievers. How can righteousness be a partner with wickedness? How can light live with darkness?" (2 Corinthians 6:14). The excitement of love and attraction is wonderful, but don't let it cloud your vision of only marrying someone who shares your faith. Better to stay single than to labor alone in a marriage that doesn't share a heart of worship for the one who created marriage.

I hope you feel the tender, spiritual, and passionate emotion found in Elizabeth Barrett Browning's sonnet about delight in one's beloved:

> How do I love thee? Let me count the ways.
> I love thee to the depth and breadth and height
> My soul can reach, when feeling out of sight
> For the ends of Being and ideal Grace.
> I love thee to the level of every day's
> Most quiet need, by sun and candlelight.
> I love thee freely, as men strive for Right;
> I love thee purely, as they turn from Praise.
> I love thee with the passion put to use
> In my old griefs, and with my childhood's faith.
> I love thee with a love I seemed to lose
> With my lost saints,—I love thee with the breath,
> Smiles, tears, of all my life!—and, if God choose,
> I shall but love thee better after death.[9]

CHAPTER 17

OUR CHILDREN

Children are a gift from the Lord;
they are a reward from him.

PSALM 127:3

PSALM 127, WRITTEN BY SOLOMON, is one of the most beautiful chapters in the Bible for parents. I love how *The Message* translates these verses:

> If God doesn't build the house,
>   the builders only build shacks.
> If God doesn't guard the city,
>   the night watchman might as well nap.
> It's useless to rise early and go to bed late,
>   and work your worried fingers to the bone.
> Don't you know he enjoys
>   giving rest to those he loves?
>
> Don't you see that children are God's best gift?
>   the fruit of the womb his generous legacy?
> Like a warrior's fistful of arrows
>   are the children of a vigorous youth.
> Oh, how blessed are you parents,
>   with your quivers full of children!

Your enemies don't stand a chance against you;
you'll sweep them right off your doorstep.

Psalm 127:1–5 THE MESSAGE

Mark and I often comment that apart from becoming Christians and getting married, having our kids has been by far the greatest experience of our lives. And since then, all of the best experiences in our lives have been done with a baby on the hip! Now with grandchildren, family life is busy but so very fulfilling.

Billy Graham said this:

> The family should be a closely knit group. The home should be a self-contained shelter of security; a kind of school where life's basic lessons are taught; and a kind of church where God is honored; a place where wholesome recreation and simple pleasures are enjoyed.[1]

I love everything he says in that word of truth, but let me highlight that little phrase "a kind of church where God is honored."

Solomon has much to say about children throughout his writings. One of his most famous proverbs instructs parents: "Direct your children onto the right path, and when they are older, they will not leave it" (Proverbs 22:6). He is echoing what Moses declared as God's spokesman on the importance of training our children in God's Word, in putting God at the center of our home, and in savoring our children as God's most precious gift to us:

> Listen, O Israel! The Lord is our God, the Lord alone. And you must love the Lord your God with all your heart, all your soul, and all your strength. And you must commit yourselves wholeheartedly to these commands that I am giving you today. Repeat them again and again to your children. Talk about them when you are at home and when you are on the road, when you are going to bed and when you are getting up. Tie them to your hands and wear them on your forehead

as reminders. Write them on the doorposts of your house and on your gates.

Deuteronomy 6:4-9

Worship God in and with and through your family. Make sure God is the center of your family life. Bless your children by teaching them God's Word. Make following Jesus the family priority, part of your own family creed.

CHERISHING AS A WITNESS TO THE WORLD

Most parents love and cherish their children. Almost all parents of faith understand their children are a gift from God. But let's not take that for granted. These verses we have read in Deuteronomy, Psalms, and Proverbs are a stark contrast to how children were viewed in Old Testament and Roman times.

The father was the absolute authority and could punish his children in whatever way he saw fit, including selling them into slavery, cutting off their fingers, or even killing them. Many religions practiced child sacrifice. Throughout the Old Testament we read of Molech, the pagan Canaanite god who demanded child sacrifice. In Leviticus 18:21, it was clear that God's people were to separate themselves from such evil practices: "Do not permit any of your children to be offered as a sacrifice to Molech, for you must not bring shame on the name of your God. I am the Lord." The Moabites, another neighbor of Israel, routinely sacrificed their children to Chemosh. Is it any wonder he was referred to as an abomination by biblical writers (see 1 Kings 11:7)?

Why did God allow the Assyrians to scatter the northern kingdom of Israel? Nothing grieved and angered Him more than their descent into the ways of surrounding nations, even to the point of sacrificing their children:

They threw out everything God, their God, had told them, and replaced him with two statue-gods shaped like bull-calves and then a phallic pole for the whore goddess Asherah. They worshiped cosmic forces—sky gods and goddesses—and frequented the sex-and-religion shrines of Baal. They even sank so low as to offer their own sons and daughters as sacrificial burnt offerings! They indulged in all the black arts of magic and sorcery. In short, they prostituted themselves to every kind of evil available to them. And God had had enough. God was so thoroughly angry that he got rid of them, got them out of the country for good until only one tribe was left —Judah.

2 Kings 17:16-19 THE MESSAGE

Was this the norm? For God's people it was the exception— and crystal clear evidence of how far they had fallen from worshiping God.

The Greeks and Romans were nearly as harsh to their children as the tribes and nations of the ancient Near East were during Old Testament days. If a baby was born with a birth defect, it was common to take the child outside the city and let it die at the hands of the elements:

An infant could be abandoned without penalty or social stigma for many reasons, including an anomalous appearance, being an illegitimate child or grandchild or a child of infidelity, family poverty, parental conflict (*ob discordiam parentum*) or being one of too many children. Sometimes they were given to friends, but more often than not they were abandoned to the elements, and death resulted from hypoglycemia and hypothermia. Sometimes the infant was devoured by the dogs that scavenged public places. It was likely however, that the *expositi* were rescued from these fates and picked up by slavers. Abandonment generally occurred in a public place, where it was hoped that the infant could be taken up by some wealthy person.[2]

It is painful to read those words, and sadly, there are still children all over the world who are not cherished. Some are sold into slavery. Some are abandoned. Some are abused. Some are killed before they are born. The mistreatment of children, whether big and grotesque or seemingly small, is a sure way to anger God.

Devout Jewish parents in Jesus' lifetime understood children were a gift from God, but Jesus took this understanding a step further when He rebuked His disciples for pushing the children to the side because they were getting in the way of grown-ups.

> One day some parents brought their children to Jesus so he could lay his hands on them and pray for them. But the disciples scolded the parents for bothering him. But Jesus said, "Let the children come to me. Don't stop them! For the Kingdom of Heaven belongs to those who are like these children." And he placed his hands on their heads and blessed them before he left.
>
> Matthew 19:13-15

This was a world-changing point of view in much of Western culture:

> It wasn't really until Christianity took hold that things changed for Roman children. Christianity taught that children were gifts from God, and therefore harm to a child was a violation of God's will. Gradually, Christian Roman emperors increased the penalties for abandoning children, they limited the number of years a child could be enslaved to five years.[3]

Worshiping God is aligning our hearts with His heart, our thoughts to His thoughts, our will to His will. Our views on children are a key way we are aligned with God's Word. Let's never grow dull to the plight of children all over the world, children that are growing up without being loved and cherished. Whatever breaks God's heart must break our heart. And the heartbreaking truth is that millions of children across the world are suffering, whether from physical and sexual abuse at home or sex trafficking or forced labor or other atrocities. You can learn more from

Compassion International at www.compassion.com/poverty/child-abuse.htm.

We love and cherish our own children, but we are also called to love and cherish all the children of the world. As you consider the plight of children today, ask Him how He might use you as a blessing to those who are most vulnerable.

As you worship God and establish worship in your family, declare with all your heart: "My children are God's precious gift to me. They are precious in His sight; they are precious in my sight." Never take for granted that your children are a gift from God. And I encourage you to always pray for the precious kids who are crying out to God from wherever they are, asking for someone to come and intervene in their seemingly hopeless situation. You just never know how God will use you and your family to bless someone else.

OUR ACTIONS AND WORDS TEACH

Children learn through our words and our actions. If you want to teach them to love God with all their heart, soul, strength, and spirit, let them see that in your life. Let them see you worship God at church with joy and enthusiasm. Let them see you pray at home, singing hymns and worship songs, and worshiping your heavenly Father in everyday life. I love that every morning, when my daughter Zoe comes downstairs for breakfast, her dad is on the couch, reading the Word of God, taking the first part of his day every day to put first things first.

I will never forget being in a seminar in which the great Australian football coach Wayne Bennett was speaking. He said that in all his years of parenting and coaching, the three strongest ways to raise champion children were 1) Example, 2) Example, 3) Example. Children may not always do as you say, but they will eventually do as they see.

In Psalm 101:1-2 David says,

I will sing of your love and justice, Lord.
  I will praise you with songs.
I will be careful to live a blameless life—
  when will you come to help me?
I will lead a life of integrity
  in my own home.

Are you modeling integrity in your own home?
Charles Spurgeon said,

> Let no Christian parents fall into the delusion that the Sunday-
> school is intended to ease them of their personal duties. The
> first and most natural condition of things is for Christian par-
> ents to train up their own children in the nurture and admo-
> nition of the Lord.[4]

When our kids were younger, we always had a favorite Bible
story book. As they moved into the teen years, it was harder to
find material that exactly fit everyone's needs for devotions. But
there is so much great material available now, and even having
your kids receive a daily reading on the family computer is a
great start. God's Word is relevant to all ages at all times. It will
take your commitment, but the fruit will be realized throughout
their lives.

THE TABLE

In Luke 22 we read that before His suffering and death, Jesus gathered His disciples to break bread with Him at the table, that common and comforting center of many homes.

That's where Jesus wanted to spend His last hours of
fellowship:

> "Go and prepare the Passover meal, so we can eat it
> together." . . . Jesus and the apostles sat down together at the
> table. Jesus said, "I have been very eager to eat this Passover
> meal with you before my suffering begins. For I tell you now

that I won't eat this meal again until its meaning is fulfilled in the Kingdom of God."

vv. 8, 14-16

It is during this meal that Jesus teaches and challenges and comforts. He models the Lord's Supper, a time when the body of Christ is to remember His sacrificial gift of blood and body.

He didn't gather with them at the temple or in a synagogue, but just in an ordinary room, eating together at the table.

The table is a common, everyday place. I think that's why it is so important to gather there as a family. It is a place to be nourished, to work, to laugh, and to fellowship. Over the years, my kitchen table has been filled with sewing machines, painting, coloring books, song lyrics, Mixmasters, cookbooks, women's magazines, and more homework than you'd ever like to imagine. But what I've loved is that it is where we have learned how to work together as a family; it is where we've learned how to open our hearts to one another through laughter and tears. If my table could speak, it would surely tell tales about what has transpired upon it over the years: writing countless invitations, addressing hundreds of envelopes, poring over all kinds of cookbooks, making great meals, making terrible meals—and all the while that table has been a classroom for teaching and a sanctuary for our hearts.

Whether you are talking about finding a space for your kids, your friends, or your spouse, it is so beneficial to find a place where there can be vulnerability and openness and honesty, without the pressure of requiring a perfect answer or the need for an immediate rebuttal. A family needs a place where they have permission to be themselves with each other. The kitchen table can be a beautiful thing. Gather together there every chance you can. Try your best to have meals together—with no television or other distractions. Just you and yours. Have a *no phones* policy at the kitchen table. My dear friend Susan has a phone bowl on her kitchen table where all the phones go—no exceptions. It's amazing what you learn about your children over an unhurried meal with no distractions. Make the time.

Let me add this about the table: Have guests in your home—practice hospitality—and include them with your children at the table. Don't send the kids away. If you need to, get a bigger table. I want my children to hear conversations about faith and God. Who knows? There may be a time when, despite my best efforts, they don't feel they can talk to me. I want them surrounded by other Christian people who love and worship God—and who might be the ones they can talk to about a particular question.

And it's great to have a culture in your home where worship music is played, and that the atmosphere you create is one of faith, not just one where the news channel blares bad news into your home every moment of every day. I heard someone describe CNN the other day as "constant negative news." This may be a bit harsh, but you get the drift!

Pastor and Bible commentator Matthew Henry said, "They that pray in the family do well; they that pray and read the Scriptures do better; but they that pray, and read, and sing do best of all."[5] No less than Charles Spurgeon often referenced his admiration for the Henry household.

A couple of years ago when my granddaughter Ava was a toddler, she had one of those days when she was being fussy. Nothing was making her happy, and even though she's normally an absolute angel, she was letting the world know she was displeased with it. I watched with wonder as my daughter Amy stopped what she was doing, knelt down at Ava's level face-to-face, and had a soft conversation with her in beautiful soothing tones. Ava calmed down, gave her momma a big smile and cuddle, and continued her day at peace with the world.

I couldn't hear all the words, but I was impressed and inspired by Amy and her mothering methods. I told Amy how proud I was of her as a mom and asked her how she was able to respond to Ava so lovingly and calmly.

Her quick answer was so poignant to me, even now. She said: "I just stop the world for her, Mom. It's just her in that moment."

I was so proud. I was so challenged. She stopped the world for her toddler and her toddler felt it.

As we cherish our children, let's not forget two things I watched my daughter do with Ava: One, we need to get down on their level—face-to-face—and interact with them with real understanding. And two, we must also get in the moment with them, where they aren't an annoyance or afterthought, but absolutely seen and heard. In other words, we need to focus on them. There are many ways to define love, but with kids, I firmly believe the adage that kids spell the word *love* with the letters T-I-M-E.

OUR PARENTS

If you grew up in a godly and loving home, thank God. If you didn't, you can still model worship of God for your own children by how you honor your own parents. The fifth commandment tells us: "Honor your father and mother. Then you will live a long, full life in the land the Lord your God is giving you" (Exodus 20:12).

It sits in such an interesting place in the Ten Commandments. The first four commandments are clearly about worship and honoring God. We are to have no other gods; we are not to worship graven images; we are not to disrespect the name of God; we are to keep the Sabbath holy.

The last five commandments are clearly about how we are to honor and get along with others: don't murder; don't commit adultery; don't steal; don't bear false witness; don't covet. But the fifth command is a bit of both. We are to honor—the word for "worship"—our parents. And it is the only commandment with a blessing. It says that as we honor our parents, we are rewarded with a long, peaceful life. I praise God that even for those who feel they cannot honor their own parents, the cross of Christ and

His finished work make it possible to stand in His grace and find strength for the impossible

Richard Blackaby writes:

> Scripture is clear we are to honor our mother and father (Exodus 20:12; Deuteronomy 5:16; Ephesians 6:2). In fact, this is the only one of the Ten Commandments that comes with a promise of blessing if we do it. The question is often asked, "But what if my parents aren't honorable? What if they hurt or betrayed me?" The Bible doesn't qualify which parents are deserving of honor. It just says to honor them.
>
> As parents get older, sometimes they can be frustrating. They get set in their ways. They can disagree with what we are doing or how we are rearing our kids. We may remember times our parents disappointed us or failed to be there for us. Everyone has these memories.
>
> There is no question some parents have inflicted great pain on their children. I would never minimize the suffering people have endured at the hands of dysfunctional parents. Yet I also know that to truly be a person of grace, you can't pick and choose those to whom you give it to. The more I come to see myself as God sees me, and I realize the magnitude of God's grace toward me every day, the easier it is to see my parents through eyes of grace.[6]

In the chapter on marriage we discussed that there are times we honor our spouse even though they aren't honorable—but we do it unto God as worship to Him. When we honor our spouse, we help our kids obey this command to honor their parents—to honor you. We instill a respect that will spill over to respect for God. We do the same thing when we honor our parents.

OUR HEAVENLY FATHER

In Ephesians 6, Paul has a word of counsel for fathers in particular: "Fathers, do not provoke your children to anger by the way you treat them. Rather, bring them up with the discipline and instruction that comes from the Lord" (Ephesians 6:4). Unfortunately, there are many children in the world who grow up without the love of a father. When there is divorce in the home, it is most common for the father to leave. This is traumatic for children. It feels like they are being divorced too. So the Scripture that tells us God loves us like a father doesn't always resonate with those who come from broken families.

Fathers, one of your biggest jobs is to not make it difficult for your children to respond to the love of their heavenly Father. Hug your children. Encourage your children. Get your kids outside to kick a ball, build a fort, make mud pies. Include them in your work at home, as it gives them a sense of ownership and accomplishment. Young women who never receive love from their natural fathers often go looking for it elsewhere, ending up in dysfunctional relationships and unhealthy codependent partnerships. Make it easy for their hearts to leap with joy at the thought of God's great love.

A COMMITMENT

Joshua made his decision and committed to it. Worried that some of God's children were wavering in their faith, he laid it out as a challenge:

> "But if serving the Lord seems undesirable to you, then choose for yourselves this day whom you will serve, whether the gods your ancestors served beyond the Euphrates, or the gods of the Amorites, in whose land you are living. But as for me and my household, we will serve the Lord."
>
> **Joshua 24:15** NIV

In Psalm 96:7 David says, "Give to the Lord, O families of the peoples, give to the Lord glory and strength" (NKJV). Charles Spurgeon had so many keen insights on family worship that I wish I could just add all he had to say. But take to heart these few highlights:

Happy is the household where the altar burns day and night with the sweet perfume of family worship![7]

Every house should be the house of God, and there should be a church in every house.[8]

Let us be cheerful and happy at family worship. In your private devotions you should also "Serve the Lord with gladness."[9]

Cherish your children; they are a gift from God. Bless them as you worship God as a family.

CHAPTER 18

IN HIS SANCTUARY

Because of your unfailing love,
I can enter your house; I will worship
at your Temple with deepest awe.

PSALM 5:7

I DON'T KNOW OF A PERFECT CHURCH. I know some reading this have had negative experiences in churches, where self-service, judgmentalism, and anger were seen more than praise, joy, and kindness. But, my friend, even if no single church has exhibited all the qualities God wants at all times and in all ways, it is still His will for us to gather together—with eagerness and enthusiasm and love. Far too many people who count themselves followers of Jesus Christ have become much too careless in their church attendance, missing out on worshiping as part of the body of Christ—voices, hearts, and hands raised *together* in exaltation of the one who is worthy!

It's boring.

I'm not being fed.

I'm so busy that I need a day that is all mine.

People aren't nice to me.

I pray that none of these statements reflect your experience, but even if you feel some of those things, you need to be in church.

Even if it's not perfect. And let's grow up about that. We all know that humans, even redeemed and sold-out-to-Christ Christians, aren't perfect. We don't always get it right. We need to get our perspective fixed; we need forgiveness and to be forgiving. So it shouldn't surprise us that no church is perfect.

Charles Spurgeon had such a way of putting things in perspective. He said this of the church:

> If I had never joined a church till I had found one that was perfect, I should never have joined one at all; and the moment I did join it, if I had found one, I should have spoiled it, for it would not have been a perfect church after I had become a member of it. Still, imperfect as it is, it is the dearest place on earth to us.[1]

This is so true! Though church is made up of flawed human beings, let me remind you that wherever God invites you to be is exactly where you need to be—and it is wonderful, the dearest place on earth!

I'm a church girl. That's where I found Jesus. And though I experience God in so many ways and so many places, to be perfectly honest, I sense His presence in my life most fully as I meet with people who love Jesus and love me; as I lift my hands and voice in praise to Him; as I soak in the teaching of His Word; as I laugh, cry, hug, and pray with others, sharing their joys and sorrows.

Saint Cyprian said, "He who does not have the church as his mother does not have God as his Father."[2] Wow. That is a strong statement. But I hear where he was coming from.

Joel Osteen says much the same thing when he comments, "You can be committed to church but not committed to Christ, but you cannot be committed to Christ and not committed to church."[3]

I pray that you find a church that becomes the dearest place on earth to you. If church isn't a place of joy and worship—if you've given up going or drag your feet every step of the way to the front door—go to God in prayer right now. Put this book down. Seek His face and guidance. Ask Him:

- Is there some past hurt I am holding on to that is keeping me from your sanctuary?

- Is there a sin or attitude in my life that is blocking me from experiencing you in the fellowship of the church?

- Am I going to church for selfish reasons, thinking only of what I want and not what you want and others need?

- How can I be a contributor in my church family rather than just a consumer?

If your heart is clean, only then should you ask God, "Am I in the right church? Is my place of worship focused on lifting you up and opening your Word?"

GATHERED AND SCATTERED

John Calvin said, "The church is the gathering of God's children, where they can be helped and fed like babies and then guided by her motherly care, grow up to manhood in maturity of faith."[4] When I think of what the church has meant to me—people who wrapped their arms around a teenaged girl who desperately needed to feel loved, friends I can share burdens and joys with, a place of spiritual energy where God's love and presence washes over me as I come to Him in worship—I am so thankful for the seasons I was fed like a baby, then guided by motherly care, and pushed to grow into maturity.

We've already described worship as breathing in the chapter on service. His presence fills us and energizes us, and as we exhale, we serve, we declare His greatness, and we walk obediently in His Spirit. Our relationship with the church is also a loving, breathing process. *Eklesia*, the Greek word for "church," means we are *called* to gather. We gather for the joy of fellowship, for hearing God's voice and instruction through the proclamation of His Word and through the Spirit working inside us, and to worship. But like Peter, James, and John, after experiencing the glory of God in the transfiguration—a literal appearance by Moses and Elijah (see Matthew 17:1-13)—we must come down from the mountain and leave the blessed fellowship, sharing the strength and wisdom we have received.

As essential as gathering is, we must also scatter if we are to be light and salt in our world (see Matthew 5:13-16). Something incredible happens when we gather. In Acts 2:1 we read: "On the day of Pentecost all the believers were meeting together in one place." Isn't that a wonderful and powerful way to describe what it means to gather as a church? We are together with one heart in *one place*. That is exactly what God wants. And what He did on that day was truly miraculous:

> On the day of Pentecost all the believers were meeting together in one place. Suddenly, there was a sound from heaven like the roaring of a mighty windstorm, and it filled the house where they were sitting. Then, what looked like flames or tongues of fire appeared and settled on each of them. And everyone present was filled with the Holy Spirit and began speaking in other languages, as the Holy Spirit gave them this ability.
>
> Acts 2:1-4

We learn so much about the transforming power of God through the life of Peter, the rock. Passionate and energetic, he was so eager to serve His Lord. But he sometimes bungled things. All of us can relate to him in his failings. In Acts 1, the passage leading up to the triumphant day of Pentecost, we discovered and noted that instead of waiting for the Spirit as Jesus commanded him, Peter acted in the flesh to select a twelfth apostle to take the place of Judas. In so doing, he created disunity.

But look at Peter after the coming of the Spirit! He stands tall, bold, fearless, eloquent, and persuasive in a heart-stirring sermon that leads to three thousand new followers of Christ (see

Acts 2:41). But he was just getting started. In chapters 3 and 4, he preaches again and even more are saved:

> While Peter and John were speaking to the people, they were confronted by the priests, the captain of the Temple guard, and some of the Sadducees. These leaders were very disturbed that Peter and John were teaching the people that through Jesus there is a resurrection of the dead. They arrested them and, since it was already evening, put them in jail until morning. But many of the people who heard their message believed it, so the number of believers now totaled about 5,000 men, not counting women and children.
>
> Acts 4:1-4

That's powerful preaching. How did it happen? Peter went to church, where there was one heart and everyone was in one place. God loves to go to work there! It doesn't even have to be a large group. Jesus tells us, "For where two or three gather together as my followers, I am there among them" (Matthew 18:20).

When the gathering is good, the scattering is powerful to spread the love of Christ. Now, our early brothers and sisters in Christ were not scattered because the lights had been turned off and the doors locked. They were scattered by persecution: "Meanwhile, the believers who had been scattered during the persecution after Stephen's death traveled as far as Phoenicia, Cyprus, and Antioch of Syria" (Acts 11:19). The gospel caught fire because the early Christians were on fire for God, and nothing—not the threat of death or prison or punishment—was going to stop them. They caught on fire at church!

I want to add one little thought about God's providence here. The brilliant ways He works out His plans are amazing. The early believers gathered and experienced God. They scattered and the church grew. At the beginning, the scattering was due to persecution. Who was the most famous persecutor? Saul of Tarsus, the man we know as Paul: "Meanwhile, Saul was uttering threats with every breath and was eager to kill the Lord's followers" (Acts 9:1).

When Paul encountered the risen Lord, he was called to be an apostle, specifically the Apostle to the Gentiles. God's plan was to use him as His ambassador to the world. But if you think about it, even in his days as an enemy of Jesus, even as a persecutor, he was helping spread the gospel to the very places he would go as an evangelist in the years to follow. What is God up to in your life?

How is He using your past and present to do a mighty work?

A SANCTUARY FROM THE STORMS

The writer to the Hebrews admonishes us: "Let us think of ways to motivate one another to acts of love and good works. And let us not neglect our meeting together, as some people do, but encourage one another, especially now that the day of his return is drawing near" (Hebrews 10:24-25).

What is the approaching day that the writer refers to? Is it judgment day? Is it a day of tribulation? I believe it is the latter, because the writer goes on in chapter 11 to describe those heroes of our faith who withstood tribulation.

I live in a safe and beautiful spot in a relatively safe country. Many readers have the same experience. But we have brothers and sisters all over the world who are suffering for their faith. According to Open Doors, an international Christian group that works in more than sixty countries, "an estimated 100 million Christians worldwide are persecuted"[5] in over sixty-five countries. The three worst offenders right now are North Korea, Somalia, and Iraq. Open Doors further reports that each month, 322 Christians are killed for their faith, 214 churches are destroyed, and 772 acts of violence are committed against Christians. All this was reported before the rise of ISIS in Syria!

Who is to say we who live in countries where there is freedom of worship won't suffer persecution ourselves? Jesus was very clear that God has many enemies who are intent on snuffing out the faith: "Then you will be arrested, persecuted, and killed.

You will be hated all over the world because you are my followers" (Matthew 24:9).

But don't let these brutal realities put fear in you. You have divine protection. The church is a sanctuary and haven against storms. Chuck Colson said, "The church is the only institution supernaturally endowed by God. It is the one institution of which Jesus promised that the gates of hell will not prevail against it."[6]

Martin Luther understood this when he penned a hymn that has echoed in the hearts of believers for centuries:

> And though this world, with devils filled, should threaten
> to undo us,
> We will not fear, for God hath willed His truth to triumph
> through us:
> The Prince of Darkness grim, we tremble not for him;
> His rage we can endure, for lo, his doom is sure,
> One little word shall fell him.
>
> That word above all earthly powers, no thanks to them,
> abideth;
> The Spirit and the gifts are ours through Him who with us
> sideth:
> Let goods and kindred go, this mortal life also;
> The body they may kill: God's truth abideth still,
> His kingdom is forever.[7]

The essential point of the call to gather in Hebrews 10 is that we honor the habit of meeting together in order to spur one another on to love and good deeds, facing whatever storms come our way together in victory. We really do need each other for safety and encouragement. When I walked through the valley of breast cancer, I don't know how I would have made it without the love of God, my family, and my church family, local and global. Remember that we are His church. The body of Christ. His gathered expression on the earth. We fuel as we gather, readied to *go* and *be* the light of Christ wherever we place our feet. We don't *go* to church; we *are* the church.

PREPARE YOUR HEART

I love the beauty of preparation for God's house. In the practical and in the spiritual. The Bible tells us to enter the sanctuary with . . .

- Peace: "If you enter your place of worship and, about to make an offering, you suddenly remember a grudge a friend has against you, abandon your offering, leave immediately, go to this friend and make things right. Then and only then, come back and work things out with God" (Matthew 5:23 The Message).

- Anticipation: "For I am about to do something new. See, I have already begun! Do you not see it? I will make a pathway through the wilderness. I will create rivers in the dry wasteland" (Isaiah 43:19).

- His Word: "How sweet your words taste to me; they are sweeter than honey" (Psalm 119:103). "Your word is a lamp to my feet and a light to my path" (Psalm 119:105 NKJV).

- Prayer: "Don't worry about anything; instead, pray about everything. Tell God what you need, and thank him for all he has done. Then you will experience God's peace, which exceeds anything we can understand. His peace will guard your hearts and minds as you live in Christ Jesus" (Philippians 4:6-7). Pray for those who are dear to you at church as well: "Timothy, I thank God for you—the God I serve with a clear conscience, just as my ancestors did. Night and day I constantly remember you in my prayers" (2 Timothy 1:3).

- Love and unity: "Your love for one another will prove to the world that you are my disciples" (John 13:35).

- Thanksgiving: "Enter his gates with thanksgiving; go into his courts with praise. Give thanks to him and praise his name" (Psalm 100:4).

Yes, preparation is essential. What we bring as His church will in a large measure determine what we experience as we gather. God is present. He is ready. Are *you*? Let God fill you with His Spirit. Let your heart find its courage, your mind find its wisdom, your will find its obedience. And be ready to worship as God desires.

I love the testimonies of those who discovered real worship throughout the history of the church. As you enter the sanctuary, turn your heart from the cares of the world to praise. The Puritan writer George Swinnock put it so quaintly but powerfully:

Prepare to meet thy God, O Christian! betake thyself to thy chamber on this Saturday night, confess and bewail thine unfaithfulness under the ordinances of God; shame and condemn thyself for thy sins, entreat God to prepare thy heart for, and assist it in, thy religious performances; spend some time in consideration of the infinite majesty, holiness, jealousy, and goodness, of that God, with whom thou art to have to do in sacred duties; ponder the weight and importance of his holy ordinances; meditate on the shortness of the time thou hast to enjoy Sabbaths in; and continue musing till the fire burneth; thou canst not think the good thou mayest gain by such forethoughts, how pleasant and profitable a Lord's day would be to thee after such preparation. The oven of thine heart thus baked in, as it were, overnight, would be easily heated the next morning; the fire so well raked up when thou wentest to bed, would be the sooner kindled when thou shouldst rise. If thou wouldst thus leave thy heart with God on the Saturday night, thou shouldst find it with him in the Lord's Day morning.[8]

Are you willing to kindle and feel the fire of His Spirit? Don't wait for the alarm clock to buzz on Sunday morning. Don't wake up and "see how you feel." Make time for the things that are important to you. Get your heart and spirit ready! God's house is one of His great priorities.

In Psalm 22, David is again beset on all sides by his enemies. In verse 1 he speaks the haunting words that would be echoed by Jesus on the cross (see Matthew 27:46): "My God, my God, why have you abandoned me? Why are you so far away when I groan for help?" (Psalm 22:1).

Have you ever cried to God and heard nothing in return? Don't despair. He hears your every word and cry. The mood of this Psalm changes dramatically when David gives voice to his praise in the presence of his brothers and sisters. Worship changes everything—its power is magnified in the sanctuary!

> I will proclaim your name to my brothers and sisters.
>> I will praise you among your assembled people.
> Praise the Lord, all you who fear him!
>> Honor him, all you descendants of Jacob!
>> Show him reverence, all you descendants of Israel!
> For he has not ignored or belittled the suffering of the needy.
>> He has not turned his back on them,
>> but has listened to their cries for help.
>
> I will praise you in the great assembly.
>> I will fulfill my vows in the presence of those who
>> worship you.
> The poor will eat and be satisfied.
>> All who seek the Lord will praise him.
>> Their hearts will rejoice with everlasting joy.
> The whole earth will acknowledge the Lord and return to
>> him.
>> All the families of the nations will bow down before him.
> For royal power belongs to the Lord.
>> He rules all the nations.
>
> Let the rich of the earth feast and worship.
>> Bow before him, all who are mortal,
>> all whose lives will end as dust.

Our children will also serve him.

> Future generations will hear about the wonders of the Lord.

His righteous acts will be told to those not yet born.

> They will hear about everything he has done.

Psalm 22:22-31

What a gathering of praise! It is done in the *assembly*, it echoes into the *whole earth*, and it transforms all that hear the sound. The poor are fed, its power echoes into the lives of our *children*, and it echoes to *future generations*. That's the immediate and enduring power of worshiping together! That's what our worship is to be.

Come to the sanctuary. Gather to draw strength. Gather to encourage others. Gather to praise your heavenly Father. Be in that one place with one heart. Gather to give. Gather to receive. Recapture the spirit *of* and *for* the church Paul called for:

> You were all called to travel on the same road and in the same direction, so stay together, both outwardly and inwardly. You have one Master, one faith, one baptism, one God and Father of all, who rules over all, works through all, and is present in all. Everything you are and think and do is permeated with Oneness.

Ephesians 4:4-6 THE MESSAGE

This is when we experience the power of heaven released over us all! In 2 Chronicles 20, the enemies of Judah had gathered in force. The Moabites and the Ammonites and many of their allies were marching against God's people. Even if we don't see armies outside our churches, we feel the animosity against God today. King Jehoshaphat of Judah felt what we feel—fear! How can we survive? How can we prevail?

Jehoshaphat called his people to prepare, asking all the people of the land to fast. Fasting? Wouldn't that make us weaker against our enemies? We need our nourishment if we are going to fight! King Jehoshaphat understood that this was not a battle that could be won in the power of human strength. The only way to be victorious would be by the might of God himself. He knew this battle was God's battle. Almost three thousand years later, nothing has changed. We don't have the strength to be victors over the forces of evil arrayed against the church today. But this is the beauty of following Christ. He *is* victorious . . . and it is through Him that we live and move and have our being.

The King meets the people in worship, gathered in the temple, reminding them of their history as he prays: "O Lord, God of our ancestors, you alone are the God who is in heaven. You are ruler of all the kingdoms of the earth. You are powerful and mighty; no one can stand against you!" (2 Chronicles 20:6). As they march to battle the next day, he declares: "Listen to me, all you people of Judah and Jerusalem! Believe in the Lord your God, and you will be able to stand firm. Believe in his prophets, and you will succeed" (v. 20).

But how does he array his armies for the battle? In a brilliant maneuver—in a formation of worship—he demonstrates his trust in God: "The king appointed singers to walk ahead of the army, singing to the Lord and praising him for his holy splendor. This is what they sang: 'Give thanks to the Lord; his faithful love endures forever!'" (v. 21).

Who leads the army? Singers! Praisers! People of worship!

As you read through this chapter of divine victory, you will discover that indeed it was God who fought and won the victory. When they reached the battlefield, not a single soldier of their enemies was left to oppose them. They were all already dead.

Oh my. Does that mean I could lead God's army? Does that mean that as we worship Him together with praise, we can be victors against anything that we must face?

My testimony is yes!

Is that your testimony? Will you gather together in one spirit and one voice in praise of the one who is worthy?

It is the untapped path to victory.

HIGH AND LIFTED UP

Lord of all the earth
And all of heaven
I come and seek Your face
Worship You with all I have within me
Humbled by Your grace

Every heart every nation
Every tribe all creation
Will bow before Your presence and sing

You are high and lifted up
You are high and lifted up
And my soul sings hallelujah
To the Lamb
The Lamb of God

Lord of righteousness
You come in glory
Bright and morning star
All my days I'll worship and adore You
Healer of my heart

Every prayer every cry
You alone satisfy
We will lift Your praise
Again and again

Majesty
Majesty
Jesus Lamb of God
Majesty
Majesty
Holy are You Lord[9]

PRIVATE WORSHIP

"But when you pray, go away by yourself,
shut the door behind you, and pray to your
Father in private. Then your Father,
who sees everything, will reward you."

MATTHEW 6:6

WE KNOW ABOUT JESUS' MIRACULOUS BIRTH. We know
He had a mother who loved Him with awe and wonder. We know
He was taken to the temple and dedicated to the Lord and recognized by two elderly precious saints. We know His family fled
to Egypt to escape the persecution of mad King Herod. We know
He grew intellectually, physically, socially, and spiritually: "Jesus
grew in wisdom and in stature and in favor with God and all the
people" (Luke 2:52). We know He was taken back to the temple on
His twelfth birthday where He blew away the religious teachers
with His wisdom and insights on Scripture: "Three days later they
finally discovered him in the Temple, sitting among the religious
teachers, listening to them and asking questions. All who heard
him were amazed at his understanding and his answers." (Luke
2:46-47).

222   Then there is silence until Jesus is thirty years of age. What
was His life like? Did He learn His earthly father's trade? Was He
outgoing? Quiet? We know for sure He learned who He was in the

Father: "For I have come down from heaven to do the will of God who sent me, not to do my own will" (John 6:38).

AFTER THE SILENCE

When it was time to reveal himself to the world, Jesus did so with power and passion and personal energy. He gave all that He was to His work. Just consider the first week we see Jesus revealed after eighteen years of silence.

John, Jesus' cousin, announces His public ministry:

> The next day John saw Jesus coming toward him and said, "Look! The Lamb of God who takes away the sin of the world! He is the one I was talking about when I said, 'A man is coming after me who is far greater than I am, for he existed long before me.'"
>
> John 1:29-30

The next day Jesus begins to gather His followers.

> The following day John was again standing with two of his disciples. As Jesus walked by, John looked at him and declared, "Look! There is the Lamb of God!" When John's two disciples heard this, they followed Jesus.
>
> John 1:35-37

On day three, Jesus attends a wedding with His mother and performs His first miracle.

> The next day there was a wedding celebration in the village of Cana in Galilee. Jesus' mother was there, and Jesus and his disciples were also invited to the celebration. . . . This miraculous sign at Cana in Galilee was the first time Jesus revealed his glory. And his disciples believed in him.
>
> John 2:1-2, 11

Jesus spends a couple days with His mother and siblings, but then heads to Jerusalem, where His public ministry will begin with a bang. Jesus introduces himself to the religious leaders in the most unforgettable of ways.

> It was nearly time for the Jewish Passover celebration, so Jesus went to Jerusalem. In the Temple area he saw merchants selling cattle, sheep, and doves for sacrifices; he also saw dealers at tables exchanging foreign money. Jesus made a whip from some ropes and chased them all out of the Temple. He drove out the sheep and cattle, scattered the money changers' coins over the floor, and turned over their tables. Then, going over to the people who sold doves, he told them, "Get these things out of here. Stop turning my Father's house into a marketplace!"
>
> John 2:13-16

What Jesus poured into the next three years is nothing short of miraculous. Just think of the energy He expended. He literally poured His life out as an offering on the cross, but He did the same thing every day leading up to it. Is it any wonder that Luke, a physician and the gospel writer who also penned Acts, notes, "But Jesus often withdrew to the wilderness for prayer" (Luke 5:16).

Jesus was all God and all man. As a man, He needed to be reenergized. That's what time alone with His Father did for Him.

If our Lord and Savior needed time to be alone with His Father, what does that say about you and me? I love the fellowship of the church. I love being with my family. I love my time in public ministry. But oh how sweet it is to pull away and spend time alone with my heavenly Father. In fact, this is the most critical of all the ways we spend our time.

If you truly want to get to know someone, you spend time alone with them. How else could Jesus, as fully man, have understood who He was in God? How could He have fully known the will of His Father?

If you would know God's will for your life, is there any other place to start than time alone with Him in His Word and in worship?

TIME AND PLACE

There are no rules on the time and place to meet with God, but I have found that it is best for me to set aside time in the morning. Every day is a new day with new challenges and opportunities. I want to start my day plugged into the Power Source for my life. I want to inhale the presence of the Spirit in order to better exhale His love and service all day. I want my will to be aligned with God from the very start. I want to tell the one who is all-worthy how much I love Him at the beginning of the day. I want to be in the front of the line to receive God's mercies that are new every morning: "The faithful love of the Lord never ends! His mercies never cease. Great is his faithfulness; his mercies begin afresh each morning" (Lamentations 3:22-23).

Corrie ten Boom said, "Don't pray when you feel like it. Have an appointment with the Lord and keep it. A man is powerful on his knees."[1]

E. M. Bounds, a spiritual giant on the subject of prayer, said this about morning prayer:

> The men who have done the most for God in this world have been early on their knees. He who fritters away the early morning, its opportunity and freshness, in other pursuits than seeking God will make poor headway seeking Him the rest of the day. If God is not first in our thoughts and efforts in the morning, He will be in the last place the remainder of the day.[2]

Of course, we are to remember God—to acknowledge and thank and praise Him—throughout the day. David loved to greet God in the morning, but He was attuned to His presence at every moment of the day, including when He lay down to sleep: "I lie awake thinking of you, meditating on you through the night" (Psalm 63:6).

Where you worship God is also up to you. Jesus taught that we are to have a private place. I think it's important that there is a time and place that is free from distractions when we bring our hearts before God. No radio. No television. No smartphone—especially no smartphone! Just you and God.

The kitchen table is a centering place in my life. It feels like sacred ground because it is where I spend time with God and family. But living on the Central Coast of Australia, I also love special times with God when I am meeting with Him in nature. The beauty of the ocean crashing against the rocky shore is such a reminder of His power and beauty and providence. And I love going to my piano and opening my Bible as I start to pray and sing. It seems like God is always waiting for me there.

Whatever time and place works best for you, the important thing is to be intentional. God is with you everywhere. But this time is special and sacred because *you* are fully present.

IN THE WORD

Many people meditate and reflect. David meditated on God's Word, saying "Oh, how I love your instructions! I think about them all day long" (Psalm 119:97); "But his delight is in the law of the Lord, and on his law he meditates day and night" (Psalm 1:2 ESV); "May my meditation be pleasing to him, for I rejoice in the Lord" (Psalm 104:34 ESV).

David was following the ancient pattern God had established for His people when He commanded: "Study this Book of Instruction continually. Meditate on it day and night so you will be sure to obey everything written in it. Only then will you prosper and succeed in all you do" (Joshua 1:8).

God's Word is alive: "For the word of God is living and active, sharper than any two-edged sword, piercing to the division of soul and of spirit, of joints and of marrow, and discerning the thoughts and intentions of the heart" (Hebrews 4:12 ESV). That's why it never grows old. We can read the same passage over and over and learn something new each time.

I love the way Joel Osteen introduces the reading of Scripture before he preaches each service. He tells the people to repeat after him: "This is my Bible. I am what it says I am. I can do what it says I can do. Today, I will be taught by the Word of God. I boldly confess: My mind is alert, my heart is receptive. I will never be the same. . . . In Jesus' name. Amen."[3]

I believe that is a fabulous declaration and attitude to take into your Bible reading each day. As part of your worship in the Word, I would like to challenge you to read the entire Bible—yes, even the Levitical code! You can start with Genesis and read through Revelation, or you can read a chapter from the Old and New Testaments each day. There are many Bible-reading plans that will help pace you. Often it is good to start on January 1 and read every day throughout the year. Or perhaps you want to focus one month on reading all of God's Word.

If God's Word is so important, we need to know what it says! All of it. I'm not suggesting that you do this every year for the rest of your days. Ha! The first time I tried a *One Year Bible* study, I felt like I should have changed the title to the *Two Year Bible*! It took me longer than I thought. Sometimes I love to read a particular book or section of Scripture slowly and with repetition. I want a more in-depth perspective. The Psalms contain the words that have taught me to worship and pierced my heart with God's majesty and unfailing love. I also have a couple of devotionals that come to my smartphone that I read each morning. The writings of others can be a wonderful way to better understand God's Word. Charles Spurgeon's extensive writings on the Psalms—*The Treasury of David*—have taught me so much and been such a help and joy to me. But don't let others have all the fun. *You* read from God's Word each day and let it speak to you.

In his sermon "Infallibility," Charles Spurgeon gave such a powerful mindset to worship God through time in the Word—pointing to Jesus' experience in the desert (emphasis added):

> How are we to handle this Sword of "It is written"? First, with
> deepest reverence. Let every word that God has spoken be Law
> and Gospel to you. Never trifle with it; never try to evade its

force or to change its meaning. God speaks to you in this Book as much as if, again, He came to the top of Sinai and lifted up His voice in thunder. I like to open the Bible and to pray, *"Lord God, let the Words leap out of the page into my soul, Yourself making them vivid, quick, powerful, and fresh to my heart."*

Our Lord Himself felt the power of the Word. It was not so much the devil who felt the power of "It is written" as Christ himself. "No," He says, "I will not command stones to be made bread; I trust in God who can, without bread, sustain Me. I will not cast Myself down from the temple; I will not tempt the Lord My God. I will not worship Satan, for God, alone, is God." The Manhood of Christ felt an awe of the Word of God and so it became a power to Him. To trifle with Scripture is to deprive yourself of its aid. Reverence it, I beseech you, and look up to God with devout gratitude for having given it to you.[4]

WORSHIP IN PRAYER

Prayer is worship because it is a confession that God not only exists but is in control. We find prayer mentioned for the first time at the end of Genesis 4. Adam and Eve had experienced Eden, perfection, but they had disobeyed God, trying to hide from Him in shame and trying to cover themselves—the outside is always a reflection of what is happening on the inside. After being expelled from the garden, experiencing separation from God, losing a child, and experiencing the joy of the birth of a grandson, man discovered the deep need to call on the name of the Lord. That hasn't changed!

The Bible is both specific and broad on the subject of prayer—we are to pray in the Spirit, to pray for each other, pray at all times, pray in silence, pray for the nations, pray for Jerusalem, pray for the sick, pray for the widows and orphans, pray with thanksgiving, pray to intercede, pray without quitting, pray with confidence, and pray in worship. The list goes on and on. Just like the body is made up of different parts—hands, feet, eyes, ears, and limbs—in a similar way, prayer consists of so many different dynamics.

As someone who truly values the worship of God in my life, I have come to understand worship and prayer are intrinsically linked. They cannot be pried apart. Revelation talks about the prayers of the saints and worship mingling together and coming before our God.

I've also come to understand that prayer is *not* some awkward moment of rhetoric reserved for public settings. Prayer is not about who is the most spiritual or eloquent. Prayer is simply talking to God. It is communication with Him about everything, thanking Him in and for everything, and bringing before Him all our requests and questions. Then we wait, looking forward to hearing Him speak to our hearts as He desires to commune with us, His children.

Prayer is not for some elect group of Christians. Prayer is for us all. Prayer beckons our hearts heavenward, toward the heart of Jesus. I love the simple eloquence of Brother Lawrence when he says, "There is not in the world a kind of life more sweet and delightful than that of a continual conversation with God."[5]

That's worship!

PERSISTENT PRAYER

A set time to worship God is wonderful. But walk *and talk* with God throughout the day. In 1 Thessalonians 5:17 we read, "Pray without ceasing" (ESV). Don't compartmentalize worship and prayer from the rest of your life. Walk with the acute awareness of God's presence each step of your day. Pray without ceasing—keep the conversation going.

In your private conversation with God, I strongly recommend that you begin stretching your spiritual muscles with the practice and discipline of intercessory prayer. Join your faith with another person's faith—or in place of their lack of faith—and ask God to move on their behalf. The best example and model of intercessory prayer is Jesus. Consider how He prays for his followers—both then and today!

> "I do not ask for these only, but also for those who will believe in me through their word, that they may all be one, just as you, Father, are in me, and I in you, that they also may be in us, so that the world may believe that you have sent me. The glory that you have given me I have given to them, that they may be one even as we are one, I in them and you in me, that they may become perfectly one, so that the world may know that you sent me and loved them even as you loved me. Father, I desire that they also, whom you have given me, may be with me where I am, to see my glory that you have given me because you loved me before the foundation of the world. O righteous Father, even though the world does not know you, I know you, and these know that you have sent me. I made known to them your name, and I will continue to make it known, that the love with which you have loved me may be in them, and I in them."
>
> **John 17:20–26** ESV

True intercessory prayer is worship because it is trust in God and love for others. It asks nothing for ourselves but seeks God's glory in the life of someone we care about. Whom do we intercede for? Pray for your church, your pastor, your country's leaders, your spouse, your parents, your children, someone who is going through a season of doubt in the wilderness, someone who is experiencing great pain, someone who has walked away from their faith, someone who is struggling in their marriage or in another significant relationship.

Prayer is part of how we help people carry the heavy burdens in their lives: "Share each other's burdens, and in this way obey the law of Christ" (Galatians 6:2). The Greek word Paul uses is translated "excessive weights." He is referring to things that are too big and heavy for one person to carry alone. A couple verses later he says each of us should carry our own backpack. Intercessory prayer is when we reach out a helping hand of faith and love and hope to someone who is buckling under their burdens.

But we pray for all the people we love and care about. Job 42:8 teaches us to pray for our friends. We pray for our enemies. We pray for our children.

Most of all we pray for His will here on earth. Jesus taught us to pray by saying:

> "Our Father in heaven,
> hallowed be your name.
> Your kingdom come,
> your will be done,
> on earth as it is in heaven.
> Give us this day our daily bread,
> and forgive us our debts,
> as we also have forgiven our debtors.
> And lead us not into temptation,
> but deliver us from evil."
>
> **Matthew 6:9-13** ESV

Wow. What a prayer. His kingdom on earth. *His kingdom.* The sound of heaven is worship, the currency of heaven is people, the presence of heaven is God's glory, majesty, and reign. The more we shine God's light over this earth, the greater impact we will have—His kingdom, heaven's reign, will be felt across the earth.

REFOCUSING OUR THOUGHT LIFE

Time alone with God is a breath of fresh air. As we align our thoughts with His thoughts through time in His Word and through prayer, our mind is renewed.

Evelyn Underhill wrote on deep spiritual truths, but always directed them to ordinary people. For her, experiencing God was available to all of us through focusing our hearts and wills. Her words convict me when she reminds us that sometimes the only thing separating us from life-changing worship is fear, laziness, and self-importance—things that are the opposite of proclaiming His worthiness in all our being:

> Eternity is with us, inviting our contemplation perpetually, but we are too frightened, lazy, and suspicious to respond; too arrogant to still our thought, and let divine sensation have its way. It needs industry and goodwill if we would make that transition; for the process involves a veritable spring-cleaning of the soul, a turning-out and rearrangement of our mental furniture, a wide opening of closed windows, that the notes of the wild birds beyond our garden may come to us fully charged with wonder and freshness, and drown with their music the noise of the gramaphone within. Those who do this, discover that they have lived in a stuffy world, whilst their inheritance was a world of morning-glory: where every tit-mouse is a celestial messenger, and every thrusting bud is charged with the full significance of life.[6]

Underhill's takeaway and challenge is simply this: "For a lack of attention a thousand forms of loveliness elude us every day."[7]

Woven throughout the pages of this book is the truth that God is present everywhere—always loving, always helping, always transforming us into the persons He wants us to be. That is never in question. The question is always, "Am I present?"

We answer this question through daily devotions, the time we spend in His Word, the time we spend in prayer—in other words, *the time we spend with Him.*

I don't want to miss any of the loveliness that God speaks into my life as I reach for Him, as I listen for Him, as I look to and for Him, and in my daily walk.

As I think of all the moments of my life, I remem
tiful thought from an unknown writer about focusir.

> Happy moments, praise God;
> Difficult moments, seek God;
> Quiet moments, worship God;
> Painful moments, trust God;
> Every moment, thank God.

CHAPTER 20

IN THE WILDERNESS

O God, you are my God; I earnestly search for you.
My soul thirsts for you; my whole body longs for you in
this parched and weary land where there is no water.

PSALM 63:1

HAVE YOU EVER BEEN IN A TIME AND PLACE in your life when you weren't sure God knew where you were or heard your prayers? Maybe it was a time of hurt or confusion or doubt.

Before Zoe was born I had a miscarriage. The loss of that baby left me filled with so much grief. Shortly after, we began a worship tour that had long been scheduled. But as we started I was still crying on the inside. I didn't think there was any way I could stand before a crowd and sing. I finally had to determine in my heart that I would sing from the depths of my soul as an act of obedience. What I discovered was that God's Spirit in me was greater than my grief.

But it wasn't easy.

Worshiping God in the wilderness isn't just for seemingly strong people, and it isn't something I want to address lightly. When we are in the wilderness, the experience is real. No two journeys will look the same or take the same amount of time to traverse. Just know that God does not leave you or reject you while you are in the desert. Last year, even on those days when I was literally just living minute by minute, I felt God in the valley with me. The darkness does not intimidate Him; He just lights it up with His greatness! He does not get mad at you for expressing sincere questions and doubts. He doesn't lose patience with you when you are confused.

LIGHT IN THE WILDERNESS

After His anointing by John the Baptist, Jesus went into the desert to be tempted. He was not driven there. He volunteered so that He could understand and relate to the times when we're tempted and feel alone. Despite having no food or drink for forty days, Jesus was well fed. How could that be? He realized His ultimate purpose was to do the will of His Father—so He found His sustenance in the words of Scripture. Jesus answered Satan's tests and temptations by quoting from God's Word, of course! Read the discourse of Matthew 4 below:

SATAN	JESUS
During that time the devil came and said to him, "If you are the Son of God, tell these stones to become loaves of bread." (v. 3)	Jesus told him, "No! The Scriptures say, 'People do not live by bread alone, but by every word that comes from the mouth of God.'" (v. 4)
Then the devil took him to the holy city, Jerusalem, to the highest point of the Temple, and said, "If you are the Son of God, jump off! For the Scriptures say, 'He will order his angels to protect you. And they will hold you up with their hands so you won't even hurt your foot on a stone.'" (vv. 5–6)	Jesus responded, "The Scriptures also say, 'You must not test the Lord your God.'" (v. 7)
Next the devil took him to the peak of a very high mountain and showed him all the kingdoms of the world and their glory. "I will give it all to you," he said, "if you will kneel down and worship me." (vv. 8–9)	"Get out of here, Satan," Jesus told him. "For the Scriptures say, 'You must worship the Lord your God and serve only him.'" (v. 10)

Is it any wonder we are to fix our eyes on Jesus, the author and perfecter of faith? He is our model in all things, including time in the wilderness. We honor Him when we do as He did—answer any confusion, temptation, loneliness, and lostness with God's Word.

David tells us that God's Word is a lamp for our feet and a light for our path. Nowhere and at no time is that more important than the rocky, rugged, tangled terrain of the wilderness. We need illumination to keep us from tumbling down a ravine; we need a bright light to ward off wild animals that would attack us in the dark; we need a map to keep us from wandering in circles like the Israelites after leaving Egypt for the Promised Land. By speaking God's words in the wilderness we find deliverance.

WORDS OF LIFE, WORDS OF DEATH

The children of Israel did have a burning light to lead them. And yet they wandered. Why? I believe it was their constant grumbling. Even after seeing God's mighty hand break the stubbornness of the pharaoh with plagues. Even after being pursued by the pharaoh's army only to miraculously be delivered by crossing the Red Sea while the Egyptian army was swallowed in the waters. They grumbled. Over and over again.

Exodus 15 tells us of a wonderful worship service. Moses leads the people in singing their hearts out in praise to God who brought them victory. They shouted with Moses: "Let God rule forever, for eternity!" (15:18 THE MESSAGE). What a celebration of joy! Miriam, Moses and Aaron's sister, led the women in a dancing march with her tambourine. They shouted, "Sing to God—what a victory! He pitched horse and rider into the sea!" (v. 21 THE MESSAGE). But their words and hearts turned negative at the first challenge they encountered. Then we read:

> Moses led Israel from the Red Sea on to the Wilderness of Shur. They traveled for three days through the wilderness without finding any water. They got to Marah, but they couldn't drink the water at Marah; it was bitter. That's why they called the

place Marah (Bitter). And the people complained to Moses, "So what are we supposed to drink?"

vv. 22-24 The Message

God provided the water they needed through Moses, but a pattern was established. "Why did you bring us out to die? What will we drink? What will we eat?" Even after God provided them exactly what they needed for daily nourishment in the form of manna, the people still grumbled and complained. They wanted meat. Nothing was to their liking.

It got so bad that these people who had seen God deliver them from the mightiest army on earth were afraid of marauding tribes that were but a speck compared to the pharaoh's forces:

> The whole community was in an uproar, wailing all night long. All the People of Israel grumbled against Moses and Aaron. The entire community was in on it: "Why didn't we die in Egypt? Or in this wilderness? Why has God brought us to this country to kill us? Our wives and children are about to become plunder. Why don't we just head back to Egypt? And right now!"

Numbers 14:1-3 The Message

We can understand their wanting to leave the wilderness, but it's difficult to imagine doing so by returning to slavery. That's exactly what their words of death were doing. The bitter grumbling had enslaved them in the wilderness. Even God could barely stand to listen to their bitter voices:

> Just then the bright Glory of God appeared at the Tent of Meeting. Every Israelite saw it. God said to Moses, "How long will these people treat me like dirt? How long refuse to trust me? And with all these signs I've done among them! I've had enough—I'm going to hit them with a plague and kill them. But I'll make you into a nation bigger and stronger than they ever were."

Numbers 14:10-12 The Message

Joyce Meyer speaks truth to us about our obedience in the wilderness: "Don't complain. The Israelites wasted forty years murmuring and complaining in the wilderness, when they could have just obeyed God and entered into their Promised Land."[1]

Thank God for a man like Moses, who interceded on behalf of this stubborn, rebellious people.

In the chapter on worshiping in the midst of suffering, we read the anguished words of David. He speaks his feelings of hurt and betrayal openly and honestly before God. But even in the midst of his anguish he never stops honoring and praising God. Our gracious heavenly Father will never tire of such confession. But when our words become poisoned and lose all sense of faith, hope, and love in Him and for Him, it's time to stop.

Jesus was our model. He spoke Scripture to His enemy, the devil. He declared God's will in the midst of hunger, thirst, temptation, trial, and every other hardship.

In the wilderness, it is a discipline to keep from continuously talking about the problem. But if we do, we keep wandering in circles long after we should have stepped into victory. Even if the feelings aren't there, we can still acknowledge God's presence with praise and thanksgiving. By God's grace, we are still to worship!

We'll talk about this more below, but let's not leave this theme of obedience too quickly. There is nothing Satan wants more than for you to fall into sin while in the wilderness. I am absolutely convinced that you and I will face our greatest temptations in these dry seasons. They may come in the form of pride, money, or promiscuity, but be assured they will come, and perhaps stronger than you've ever experienced. There is a spiritual reason for this. Since a wilderness experience always precedes key spiritual breakthroughs—a deepened, more mature, more grown-up faith; new insights into the nature of God; a new vitality to witness and minister—this is when Satan pulls out stops to block that from happening. In a sense, facing enhanced temptation is a compliment and a comfort. You have Satan's attention. He knows there's something new right around the corner for you that will glorify

God and build His kingdom. There is nothing Satan wants more than to thwart the will of God and break your fellowship with Him—and there is nothing God wants more than for you to persevere in the journey through the marvelous realization that He is with you always, even when you don't feel near Him.

In the classic book *The Screwtape Letters*, C. S. Lewis pens this note of warning from a supervising demon to a junior demon who has been given the task of sabotaging the faith of a new believer:

> Do not be deceived, Wormwood. Our cause is never more in danger than when a human, no longer desiring, but still intending, to do our Enemy's will, looks round upon a universe from which every trace of Him seems to have vanished, and asks why he has been forsaken, and still obeys.[2]

RIGHTEOUS HUNGER AND THIRST

I think it's important to note that in the wilderness we know how needy we are. Success can be much more dangerous to our spiritual vitality than a dry season. When all is going the way we want, we can grow complacent and lose the hunger and thirst that drives us into the arms of God.

In Psalm 63, David shares his experience of living in a desert wilderness, *a parched and weary land where there is no water* (see v. 1). While stumbling through life and barely surviving, David *searches, longs, and thirsts for God*. Even if it seems God is nowhere to be found—though He really is there—never lose your hunger and thirst for Him. Don't give in to the temptation to despair and give up.

What if David had given up? He was a man who knew God's heart and forged a kingdom in God's mighty name. He was a hero of faith. He brought the heart of worship to his people and to every generation that has followed through his Psalms. All because he did not quit in the desert.

David's life was not easy. He had to fight to survive at every age and stage. As a young shepherd boy sent off to tend his father's flocks in the high country, he was attacked by both a bear and a lion—and he saved himself and his sheep both times (1 Samuel 17:34-36). As an adolescent he volunteered to stand for God against the champion of the Philistines, Goliath. As a young man already anointed by Samuel to be king, he was forced to flee to the desert to survive the insane, murderous rage of King Saul (see 1 Samuel 21-23).

Make no mistake, the desert is a harsh place. No water. Unrelenting heat. For David, the desert was a place where his natural strength would be stretched to its limit. Not only was his body thirsty and hungry, but his life was in danger and fear lurked around every corner, chipping away at his emotional well-being.

What are the deserts of your life, those spaces that feel rough and full of questions, where you feel stretched to the limit, where it seems like even your faith will not sustain you? Previous spiritual and physical comforts are not available, and the prolonged season seems impossible to get through. But don't give up. There are lessons about the nature of God—the depths of His faithfulness and love—you'll only learn in the valleys of life. You'll never learn them on the mountaintop.

Jesus begins the Sermon on the Mount by redefining true happiness:

> You're blessed when you're at the end of your rope. With less of you there is more of God and his rule. You're blessed when you feel you've lost what is most dear to you. Only then can you be embraced by the One most dear to you.
>
> Matthew 5:3-4 THE MESSAGE

David experienced the depths of God's faithfulness in his desert wilderness. As we read through Psalm 63 we hear him proclaim: "O God, you are my God." Even as Saul, even as the desert, even as his doubts and disappointments and confusion closed in on him, David clung to the one thing he knew could never be taken from him: his personal relationship with God.

Even if you feel distant, I know you are close, my God. I will live with trust.

It wasn't David's parents' God he called out to. It wasn't his people's God—the one he learned about at Sunday school or in a Bible storybook. It wasn't the God he had read about or heard about in sermons. *You are my God.* David declares how close and personal and intimate he is with God and God is with him. Do you have that closeness? In your relationship with God, have you gone past knowing Him abstractly to personally? When you are in the wilderness, do you have a personal relationship you can cling to?

In declaring "You are my God," David established and determined that God was the ruler of his heart. He would trust and obey Him no matter what came.

Whatever is going on in your world today, I ask you this question: Is Jesus Lord of your life? It is one thing to be saved—to ask Christ into your heart—but there is also the journey of following Him as *King* of your heart. David understood lordship, and because of this he lived his life surrendered to God's will and purpose.

Accompanying this life of trust is great peace. There was no desert in David's heart, though there was a desolate land all around him.

EXPECT HIM

David rose early to seek God, to place his life before Him. Early in the morning, when hope is at its loudest, when newness is represented across the universe, David prayed.

Jonah waited until he was in the belly of the whale to finally cry out to God for salvation. Don't wait until the middle or the end of a harsh season to inquire of God. Pray as David prayed: *My soul thirsts, my flesh longs for you* . . . even though all I see are dead branches and dry places, where everything in and around me feels like it's taking its last breath. There is no water, but I'm looking at you, God, for your love is better than life!

For David, everything in nature looked bleak, but a great statement of faith came from within him as his spiritual hunger and thirst were satisfied, as he worshiped God: "So here I am in the place of worship, eyes open, drinking in your strength and glory" (Psalm 63:2 THE MESSAGE). He worshiped, *expecting* God's presence. He lifted his hands as an expression of adoration, reverence, and surrender. He lifted his hands as an outward sign of his faith: "Your unfailing love is better than life itself; how I praise you! I will praise you as long as I live, lifting up my hands to you in prayer" (vv. 3–4). Lifting up hands is the oldest gesture of prayer. We surrender ourselves. We step out in faith and stir up our souls (mind, will, and emotions).

When life invades your soul, it can feel very difficult to pull yourself out of the darkness. But this is where God's Spirit, already alive within us, is activated by our faith. Our spirits are rekindled by being bold in our declarations of faith, by being obedient to Scriptures. Lift up your head, lift up your hands, and worship Him. This is why David could say, "Your love is better than life," even when the world around him looked dim. Worship changes everything—even a desert wilderness becomes a place of sweet fellowship with God.

David's confession stirred his faith as he meditated on God's faithfulness rather than his situation. He said, "I will rejoice in the shadow of your wing, and my soul follows close behind you."

What do you do when your soul aches and you can't sleep or you have wakeful moments of anxiety in the night? David said that he worshiped and praised God. "I remember You upon my bed and meditate on You in the night watches" (Psalm 63:6 AMPLIFIED). As he poured out his heart in worship day and night to God, David discovered strength. His faith rose.

In the wilderness, go to the Word, meditate on the Word, and speak the Word in worship. Your hunger and thirst, your expectation that God will draw near, will be satisfied.

OBEY IN THE WILDERNESS

One of David's greatest tests in the wilderness was the clear, simple opportunity to kill his enemy. Saul had hunted David like an animal. He led a large war party to seek and destroy the object of his envy. David stayed on the move with stealth and guile—and fear.

Lo and behold, one night David crept into Saul's camp and stood above the man himself, his tormentor. In his heart, I'm sure David wanted nothing more than to slice Saul's throat. But he didn't. He left a token of his presence to let Saul know he was there. But he could not slay him. His words sound the call to obey: "The Lord forbid that I should do this to my lord the king. I shouldn't attack the Lord's anointed one, for the Lord himself has chosen him" (1 Samuel 24:6).

More than any other prophet, Isaiah saw the coming of our Lord and Savior, the Messiah, the Deliverer. What would that *Child who was born to us* do?

> Listen! It's the voice of someone shouting,
> "Clear the way through the wilderness
>> for the Lord!
> Make a straight highway through the wasteland
>> for our God!
> Fill in the valleys,
>> and level the mountains and hills.
> Straighten the curves,
>> and smooth out the rough places.
> Then the glory of the Lord will be revealed,
>> and all people will see it together.
>> The Lord has spoken!"

Isaiah 40:3-5

He clears a path through the wilderness: valleys are raised, mountains are brought low, all obstacles to salvation are removed!

When we acknowledge and worship God in the wilderness, He is there. He reveals himself and His grace abounds. These words of Isaiah are prophetic concerning the coming of Christ to save the world, but they also apply to your life, right now, today. Should you find yourself in the wilderness, Jesus Christ will save you and bring you home. He will make a way when there seems to be no way.

Charles Spurgeon's words from a sermon preached in 1893 are just as powerful and relevant to us today:

> You say, "O Sir, you do not know what my trial is!" No, I do not, but your heavenly Father does, and if He loved you when you were ungodly, will He cast you away, now that He has shed His love abroad in your heart?
>
> "Oh, but I have lost the very staff of bread! I do not know how I am to get a living." No, but you have the living God to depend upon and, after giving His Son to save you, He will surely give you bread! He will not let you famish.
>
> "Ah, but, my dear Sir, the beloved of my heart is laid low! There is, in the cemetery, the dearest object of my affection." Is it really so? I thought that He left the dead some time ago. I thought that the dearest object of your affection had gone up to the right hand of the Father. Is it not so?
>
> "Ah, that is not what I mean, Sir! I mean that I have lost one whom I fondly loved." I know that you have, but do you think that the Lord has turned against you because He has permitted this trial to come upon you? How can He ever desert those for whom He died? And if He died for them when they were ungodly, will He not live for them, now that He has shed His love abroad in their hearts by the Holy Spirit?[3]

CHAPTER 21

ETERNITY

*Then I heard again what sounded like the shout of a vast crowd
or the roar of mighty ocean waves or the crash of loud thunder:
"Praise the Lord! For the Lord our God, the Almighty, reigns.
Let us be glad and rejoice, and let us give honor to him. For the time
has come for the wedding feast of the Lamb, and his bride has prepared
herself. She has been given the finest of pure white linen to wear."*

REVELATION 19:6-8

ON THE DAY WE RESPONDED IN POSITIVE, active, obedient faith to the lavish, indescribable, magnificent offer of salvation through Jesus Christ our Lord, we began a journey of worship.

My prayer is that God, through the teaching and inner working of the Holy Spirit, will use *Worship Changes Everything* to deepen, widen, strengthen, and nourish you in worship; to help you live, love, pray, praise, work, walk, serve, give, overcome—to breathe—in the presence of God.

We have covered many miles on a variety of roads, passing many signposts and markers on our journey of worship together through this book.

We began our journey with the greatness, the majesty, the worthiness of God, discovering and realizing that His glory is at the heart of all worship. I pray that your heart will be stirred by the glory and presence of Jesus, and that with every fiber of your being you will recognize and acknowledge that He alone is worthy of all our praise.

We continued our journey by focusing on the presence of God. He is always near. Do we see Him? Do you? Do you see God in your sitting and standing; in your coming and going; before you and behind you; in your words and in your silence? Have you become aware that you are in God and God is in you? Acts 17:28 says, "For in him we live and move and have our being. As some of your own poets have said, 'We are his offspring'" (NIV). Worship is experiencing the God who is always there. It is for us to open our hearts and minds to experience that presence.

Our next stop on the journey of worship kept our focus on the nature of God, specifically on His amazing love for us. When we open our eyes and really see our Savior, the first thing we realize is just how much He loves us. He loves us so much He reaches out to us—even when we are running away from Him. That is why worship—even our obedient response in worship—is a divine miracle. In all other religions, it is man that seeks God. Through Jesus Christ, God reveals to us that out of His great love He has been seeking us.

Continuing on the road of worship, we looked at our very first response to who God is. We too easily think of worship as ritual when all along God has told us worship is relational. Worship is our response to the matchless love of Christ, and with all our heart, soul, strength, mind, and spirit we love and honor Him.

When we fall in love with God for who He really is—breathing in His glory and grace, His love, His faithfulness, His kindness, His patience—it is only natural that we breathe out expressions of praise and thanksgiving. We praise Him for who He is and thank Him for all He has done. This is how we honor God with everything we are, everything we have, and everything we do.

Worship changes everything because it invades and pervades every aspect of our lives.

It shows up in our relationships and is often characterized by how deeply we love others: the lost of the world, our neighbors, our brothers and sisters in Christ, our parents, our children, our spouses, our colleagues—even our enemies! And yes, it shows up in the love we have for ourselves. We love others so well, in part, because we love ourselves so well.

It also shows up in how we think, learning to replace fear and negativity with a faith-filled, optimistic, positive outlook on life.

It shows up in how we speak and how we act—we turn from words that tear down to words of blessing that bring encouragement into the lives of others. We now have a willingness and eagerness to serve, drawing energy from blessing others. And we turn our backs on greed and a miserly spirit to a generosity that is so comfortable in seasons of plenty and seasons of lack, knowing full well God provides everything we need.

It shows up in the various places we find ourselves in life: in the wilderness, in our alone times, and in the sanctuary.

But this leads me to one more place we will worship God.

You see, we have only just begun our journey into worship. This is just the start. Be assured, as good as worship is now, the best is yet to be.

WORSHIP IN ETERNITY

We experience God as we worship Him in the here and now. We experience heaven on earth in His presence. But a day is coming when we will experience Him in all His glory. Face-to-face. No veils. No walls. When we are with God in heaven, we will experience true light: "And the city has no need of sun or moon, for the glory of God illuminates the city, and the Lamb is its light" (Revelation 21:23).

The world God has placed us in is nothing short of miraculous, surrounded by creation and experience. Through great and hard times, moments of worship fill us with joy. Our loved ones are so dear to us. But this is only a foretaste of what is to come!

Paul tells us we are citizens of not just this world, but the heavenly realm:

But there's far more to life for us. We're citizens of high heaven! We're waiting the arrival of the Savior, the Master, Jesus Christ, who will transform our earthly bodies into glorious bodies like his own. He'll make us beautiful and whole with the same powerful skill by which he is putting everything as it should be, under and around him.

Philippians 3:20-21 The Message

When we gather to worship, hearts united, our voices raised together in love and adoration of our wonderful Lord—as good as this is, it is only a shadow, a foretaste of what we will experience in heaven:

I looked again. I heard a company of Angels around the Throne, the Animals, and the Elders—ten thousand times ten thousand their number, thousand after thousand after thousand in full song:

The slain Lamb is worthy!
Take the power, the wealth, the wisdom, the strength!
Take the honor, the glory, the blessing!

Revelation 5:11-12 The Message

As beautiful as our world is right now, it can't compare to the world that is to come. Truly heaven is a place of God's glory. It is beautiful. It is filled with joy unspeakable. I can't pretend to comprehend all the images John shares with us in Revelation 21:

And I saw the holy city, the new Jerusalem, coming down from God out of heaven like a bride beautifully dressed for her husband. . . . He will wipe every tear from their eyes, and there will be no more death or sorrow or crying or pain. All these things are gone forever. . . . It shone with the glory of God and sparkled like a precious stone—like jasper as clear as crystal. . . .

The wall was made of jasper, and the city was pure gold, as clear as glass. The wall of the city was built on foundation stones inlaid with twelve precious stones: the first was jasper, the second sapphire, the third agate, the fourth emerald, the fifth onyx, the sixth carnelian, the seventh chrysolite, the eighth beryl, the ninth topaz, the tenth chrysoprase, the eleventh jacinth, the twelfth amethyst. The twelve gates were made of pearls—each gate from a single pearl! And the main street was pure gold, as clear as glass.

VV. 2, 4, 11, 19–21

It is in worship that we catch our first glimpses of the beauty of eternity in God's presence and prepare our hearts to be there. I have sat with many people as they've battled with poor health who have said, "Thank God this is not all there is." The promise of heaven is stronger than their pain. My own father, as he was weeks away from entering into heaven, said to me, "The miracle that I know is *salvation*. Everything else is a bonus. And if I'm not physically healed on earth, know that I will be healed *soon*." This is also why I love the honor of leading others in worship, where they can enter into God's fullness for themselves, speak to Him, and have Him speak tenderly to their hearts. This is why I love leading worship in developing nations, where I can sit with the dying and declare God's promise of eternity and wholeness over them with confidence. There is no greater privilege than leading people to the love of Christ, the love that encompasses all else, the love that ultimately leads to God himself, the Alpha and Omega, the beginning and the end. I believe that heaven starts here on earth, as we bring His Kingdom reign to wherever we find ourselves.

Never worry about spending too much time thinking about heaven and eternity. As C. S. Lewis said, "If you read history you will find that the Christians who did most for the present world were precisely those who thought most of the next."[1]

Consider the impact of evangelist Billy Graham. Who has preached to more people and seen more people come to Christ? His life was nonstop service to God. But what was his view on eternity? "My home is heaven. I'm just traveling through this world."

Just as importantly, thoughts of heaven and eternity encourage and comfort us in all that we face that is not perfect today. Paul reminds us of this truth by saying, "Our Lord Jesus Christ himself and God our Father, who loved us and by his grace gave us eternal comfort and a wonderful hope" (2 Thessalonians 2:16).

Again, Paul shares the encouragement of eternity to help us endure all things at all times when he says,

> So we're not giving up. How could we! Even though on the outside it often looks like things are falling apart on us, on the inside, where God is making new life, not a day goes by without his unfolding grace. These hard times are small potatoes compared to the coming good times, the lavish celebration prepared for us. There's far more here than meets the eye. The things we see now are here today, gone tomorrow. But the things we can't see now will last forever.
>
> 2 Corinthians 4:16-18 The Message

Sir Thomas Moore put it so simply: "Earth has no sorrow that heaven cannot heal."[2]

Even if I can't comprehend or describe all that John shows us in Revelation, I know heaven is a place of perfection: no more pollution and natural disaster—creation is in harmony with the Creator; no more sin, murder, violence, strife, and grief—just love; no more illness, injury, and pain—complete, perfected, healed minds and bodies; and no more rebellion against the Creator—only full recognition and love for Him.

True perfection is being in the very presence of God. As Max Lucado says, "We may speak about a place where there are no tears, no death, no fear, no night; but those are just the benefits of heaven. The beauty of heaven is seeing God."[3]

Worship changes everything, giving us a glimpse, a taste, a whisper, a shout of the beauty and glory of eternity. Worship changes everything because it is the reality of His presence that leads us to the heavenly, forever experience of worshiping God for eternity.

I love you so much, and I praise God for each and every one of you. Let's lead as many precious people as we can in this journey of life to the love of Christ Jesus!

Forever and always,

Darlene

Darlene Zschech

NOTES

Introduction: When God Comes Close

1. Max Lucado, *God Came Near*, deluxe ed. (Nashville: Thomas Nelson, 2004), 6-7.

PART ONE: THE HEART OF WORSHIP

Chapter 1: He Is Worthy

1. Tom Wells, *A Vision for Missions* (Carlisle, PA: Banner of Truth, 1985), 23.
2. Rick Warren, *The Purpose Driven Life: What on Earth Am I Here For?* (Grand Rapids, MI: Zondervan, 2002), 18.
3. Bill Thrasher, *A Journey to Victorious Praying: Finding Discipline and Delight in Your Prayer Life* (Chicago: Moody, 2003), 208.
4. "Worthy Is the Lamb" by Darlene Zschech © 2000 Wondrous Worship (admin. by Music Services o/b/o Llano Music LLC). All Rights Reserved. Used By Permission.

Chapter 2: He Is Present

1. Brother Lawrence, *The Practice of the Presence of God: The Best Rule of Holy Life*, trans. Edgar G. Barton (London: Epworth), in "Second Conversation," http://www.ccel.org/ccel/lawrence/practice.iii.ii.html.
2. A. W. Tozer, *The Pursuit of God* (Abbotsford, WI: Aneko Press, 2015), Kindle edition.

Chapter 3: He Is Loving

1. Unknown, "I Love Him," 1908, public domain.
2. Evelyn Underhill, *The Letters of Evelyn Underhill*, ed. Charles Williams (New York: Longmans, Green, 1943), 184.
3. Evelyn Underhill, *The Making of a Mystic: New and Selected Letters of Evelyn Underhill*, ed. Carol Poston (Chicago: University of Illinois Press, 2010), 105.
4. John Newton, "Amazing Grace," 1779, public domain.
5. Brennan Manning, *The Ragamuffin Gospel* (Sisters, OR: Multnomah, 2000), 102.
6. Tullian Tchividjian, Twitter post, May 19, 2014, 8:52 a.m., https://twitter.com/PastorTullian.
7. Charlotte Elliott , "Just As I Am," 1835, public domain.

Chapter 4: His Love for Me, My Love for Him

1. Paraphrase from Philip Yancy, *Disappointment With God: Three Questions No One Asks* (Grand Rapids, MI: Zondervan, 1992), 103.
2. Francis Chan with Danae Yankoski, *Crazy Love: Overwhelmed by a Relentless God*, rev. ed. (Colorado Springs: David C. Cook, 2013), 63.

Chapter 5: My Praise to Him

1. *The Journals of Jim Elliot*, ed. Elisabeth Elliot (Grand Rapids, MI: Revell, 2002), 174.
2. Jonathan Edwards, *The Works of Jonathan Edwards*, ed. Henry Rogers, Sereno E. Dwight, Edward Hickman (London, 1839).
3. John Piper, *Desiring God: Meditations of a Christian Hedonist*, rev. ed. (Colorado Springs: Multnomah, 2011), 46.
4. Warren, *Purpose Driven Life*, 74.

Chapter 6: My Gratitude to Him

1. G. K. Chesterton, *The Collected Works of G. K. Chesterton*, vol. 10, *Collected Poetry, Part I*, ed. Aidan Mackey (San Francisco: Ignatius, 1994), 43.
2. C. H. Spurgeon, *John Ploughman's Talk; or, Plain Advice for Plain People*, 1896, The Spurgeon Archive, accessed June 12, 2015, http://www.spurgeon.org/misc/plowman.htm.
3. Warren Wiersbe, *Real Worship: Playground, Battleground, or Holy Ground?* 2nd ed. (Grand Rapids, MI: Baker, 2000), 26.
4. "A. W. Tozer Quotes," AZ Quotes, accessed June 26, 2015, http://www.azquotes.com/quote/532808.

Chapter 7: My Service

1. "Ravi Zacharias Quotes," AZ Quotes, accessed July 28, 2015, http://www.azquotes.com/quote/566481.
2. Warren, *Purpose Driven Life*, 125.
3. Billy Graham, in *The Chicago American*, April 16, 1967, quoted in William Joseph Federer, ed., *America's God and Country Encyclopedia of Quotations* (St. Louis: Amerisearch, 2000), 264.
4. Phillips Brooks, "Going Up to Jerusalem," *Twenty Sermons: Fourth Series* (New York, 1890).
5. Charles Spurgeon, "Service or Servitude—Which?" sermon, April 30, 1893.
6. James Russell Miller, *The Joy of Service* (New York, 1898).

Chapter 8: My Mission

1. William Booth, *A Vision of the Lost*, http://jesus.org.uk/christian-classics/william-booth.

Chapter 9: My Love for Others

1. Joyce Meyer, "Perfect Love Casts Out Fear," Joyce Meyer Ministries, accessed June 17, 2015, http://joycemeyer.org/articles/ea.aspx?article=perfect_love_casts_out_fear.
2. "Mother Teresa Quotes," AZ Quotes, accessed June 26, 2015, http://www.azquotes.com/quote/292121.
3. Manning, *Ragamuffin Gospel*, 162.
4. T.D. Jakes, *Let It Go: Forgive So You Can Be Forgiven* (New York: Atria Books, 2012), 33.

Chapter 10: My Attitude

1. James Allen, *The Life Triumphant: Mastering the Heart and Mind*, 1908, The James Allen Free Library, accessed June 17, 2015, http://james-allen.in1woord.nl/?text=the-life-triumphant.
2. James Allen, *As a Man Thinketh*, 1902, The James Allen Free Library, accessed June 17, 2015, http://james-allen.in1woord.nl/?text=as-a-man-thinketh.
3. "Charles R. Swindoll Quotes," GoodReads.com, accessed June 17, 2015, http://www.goodreads.com/author/quotes/5139.Charles_R_Swindoll.
4. Don Colbert, *Deadly Emotions: Understand the Mind-Body-Spirit Connection That Can Heal or Destroy You* (Nashville: Thomas Nelson, 2003), 162.
5. J. I. Packer, *Revelations of the Cross* (Peabody, MA: Hendrickson, 2013), 181.
6. John Piper, *God Is the Gospel: Meditations on God's Love as the Gift of Himself* (Wheaton, IL: Crossway Books, 2005), 47.
7. Matthew Henry, Thomas Scott, *A Commentary Upon the Holy Bible*, vol. 5 (London, 1835).

Chapter 11: My Words

1. Joyce Meyer, *Change Your Words, Change Your Life: Understanding the Power of Every Word You Speak* (New York: FaithWords, 2012), 5-7.
2. George Orwell, "Politics and the English Language," *Horizon* (April 1946), accessed June 18, 2015, http://wikilivres.ca/wiki/Politics_and_the_English_Language.
3. Widely attributed to Dean Koontz, *From the Corner of His Eye* (New York: Bantam Books, 2000), front matter. Editor's note: In his novel, Koontz attributes this quote to *This Momentous Day* by H. R. White.
4. "Dietrich Bonhoeffer Quotes," GoodReads.com, accessed June 18, 2015, http://www.goodreads.com/author/quotes/29333.Dietrich_Bonhoeffer.
5. Charles Spurgeon, *The Salt-Cellars: Being a Collection of Proverbs Together With Homely Notes Thereon*, vol. 2 (London, 1889).
6. "Shout to the Lord" by Darlene Zschech © 1993 Wondrous Worship (admin. by Music Services o/b/o Llano Music LLC). Rights Reserved. Used By Permission.

Chapter 12: Suffering

1. Rick Warren, "Problems Force Us to Depend on God," RickWarren.org, May 21, 2014, http://rickwarren.org/devotional/english/problems-force-us-to-depend-on-god.
2. "No One Like You" by Darlene Zschech.

Chapter 13: Money

1. Billy Graham, quoted in *The Leadership Secrets of Billy Graham* (Grand Rapids, MI: Zondervan, 2005), 107.

2. Charles Swindoll, "God Owns It All," Insight for Living Ministries, copyright 2010, accessed June 19, 2015, http://www.insight.org/resources/articles/stewardship/god -owns-it-all.html?.

3. John Charles Ryle, *Practical Religion: Being Plain Papers on the Daily Duties, Experience, Dangers, and Privileges of Professing Christians* (London, 1878).

4. Saint John Chrysostom (c. 349-407), *Homilies on the Gospel According to St. John.*

5. Warren, *Purpose Driven Life*, 46.

6. John Piper, *Brothers, We Are Not Professionals: A Plea to Pastors for Radical Ministry*, rev. ed. (Nashville: B&H, 2013), 201.

7. George MacDonald, *Paul Faber, Surgeon* (Philadelphia, 1879).

8. C. S. Lewis, *Mere Christianity* in *The Complete C. S. Lewis Signature Classics* (New York: HarperOne, 2002), 77.

9. "Fulton J. Sheen Quotes," AZ Quotes, accessed June 19, 2015, http://www.azquotes.com/ quote/566697.

10. "Martin Luther Quotes," AZ Quotes, accessed June 19, 2015, http://www.azquotes.com/ quote/823861.

11. John Wesley, "The Use of Money," sermon, February 17, 1744.

Chapter 14: Loving Myself

1. Abraham Lincoln, "Address on Colonization to a Deputation of Negroes," August 14, 1862.

2. Victoria Osteen, "Where Do You Get Your Value?" Joel Osteen Ministries, September 9, 2014, http://www.joelosteen.com/Pages/Blog.aspx?blogid=8978.

3. Brennan Manning, *Souvenirs of Solitude: Finding Rest in Abba's Embrace* (Colorado Springs: NavPress, 2009), 73.

4. John Ortberg, *The Me I Want to Be: Becoming God's Best Version of You* (Grand Rapids, MI: Zondervan, 2010), 165.

Chapter 15: My Work

1. "Billy Graham Quotes," AZ Quotes, accessed June 26, 2015, http://www.azquotes.com/ quote/114855.

2. "Zig Ziglar Quotes," AZ Quotes, accessed June 26, 2015, http://www.azquotes.com/ quote/325054.

3. Henry Ward Beecher, "Morning Sermon," March 11, 1860.

4. Richard Exley, *The Rhythm of Life: Putting Life's Priorities in Perspective* (Tulsa: Honor Books, 1987).

5. Martin Luther, quoted in E. M. Bounds, *Purpose in Prayer* (New Kensington, PA: Whitaker House, 1997), 22.

6. John Wesley, quoted in H. Newton Malony, *The Amazing John Wesley: An Unusual Look at an Uncommon Life* (Downers Grove, IL: InterVarsity Press, 2010), 157.

7. "Saint Francis de Sales Quotes," BrainyQuote.com, accessed June 29, 2015, http://www .brainyquote.com/quotes/quotes/s/saintfranc193320.html.

8. Dietrich Bonhoeffer, *Psalms: The Prayer Book of the Bible* (Minneapolis: Augsburg, 1970), 64-65.

9. Thomas Carlyle, *Past and Present* (London, 1843).

10. Elisabeth Elliot, *Discipline: The Glad Surrender* (Grand Rapids, MI: Revell, 1982, 2006), 126.

Chapter 16: Our Marriage

1. Max Lucado, "What God Says About Gay Marriage," Email Brigade News Report, accessed June 23, 2015, http://www.emailbrigade.com/68.html.

2. Lewis, *Mere Christianity*, 93.

3. Timothy Keller, Kathy Kellery, *The Meaning of Marriage: Facing the Complexities of Commitment with the Wisdom of God* (New York: Dutton, 2011), 96.

4. Emerson Eggerichs, "About Love & Respect Ministries," accessed June 23, 2015, http:// loveandrespect.com/about-us/.

5. Piper, *Brothers, We Are Not Professionals*, 278.

6. G. K. Chesterton, *Heretics* (London, 1905).

7. Lewis, *Mere Christianity*, 86.

8. John MacArthur, *The MacArthur New Testament Commentary: First Corinthians* (Chicago: Moody, 1984), 157.

9. Elizabeth Barrett Browning, "How Do I Love Thee?", no. 43, *Sonnets From the Portugese* (1850).

Chapter 17: Our Children

1. Billy Graham, *The Quotable Billy Graham*, ed. Cort R. Flint (Anderson, SC: Droke House, 1966), 74.
2. A. R. Colon, *A History of Children: A Socio-cultural Survey Across Millennia* (Westport, CT: Greenwood Press, 2001), 91.
3. Colon, *A History of Children*, 104.
4. Charles Spurgeon, *Come Ye Children: A Book for Parents and Teachers on the Christian Training of Children* (London, 1887).
5. Matthew Henry, quoted in Charles Spurgeon, "Praising God," *The Pulpit Treasury: An Evangelical Monthly* 4 (November 1886), 445.
6. Richard Blackaby, *Putting a Face on Grace: Living a Life Worth Passing On* (Sisters, OR: Multnomah, 2006), 90-91.
7. Charles Spurgeon, "Prayer Meetings," sermon, August 30, 1868.
8. Charles Spurgeon, "Lydia, the First European Convert," sermon, September 20, 1891.
9. Charles Spurgeon, "Serving the Lord With Gladness," sermon, September 8, 1867.

Chapter 18: In His Sanctuary

1. Charles Spurgeon, "The Best Donation," sermon, April 5, 1891.
2. Saint Cyprian, quoted in R. C. Sproul, *1-2 Peter*, St. Andrew's Expositional Commentary (Wheaton, IL: Crossway, 2011), 134.
3. "Joel Osteen Quotes," IZ Quotes, accessed June 29, 2015, http://izquotes.com/quote/140010.
4. John Calvin, *The Institutes of Christian Religion*, ed. Tony Lane, Hilary Osborne (Grand Rapids, MI: Baker Academic, 1987), 232.
5. "Persecution of Christians Reaches Historic Levels, Conditions Suggest Worst Is Yet to Come," Open Doors, January 7, 2015, https://www.opendoorsusa.org/newsroom/tag -news-post/persecution-of-christians-reaches-historic-levels-conditions-suggest-worst -is-yet-to-come/. Additional information from the "Christian Persecution" and "World Watch List" sections of www.opendoorsusa.org.
6. "Charles Colson Quotes," AZ Quotes, accessed June 25, 2015, http://www.azquotes.com/ quote/759170.
7. Martin Luther, "A Mighty Fortress Is Our God," 1529, trans. Frederic H. Hedge, 1853, public domain.
8. *The Works of George Swinnock, M.A.* vol. 1 (London, 1868).
9. "High and Lifted Up" by Darlene Zschech & Mike Guglielmucci © 2008 Wondrous Worship (admin. by Music Services o/b/o Llano Music LLC) / Hillsong Publishing (admin. by Capitol CMG Publishing). All Rights Reserved. Used By Permission.

Chapter 19: Private Worship

1. "Corrie ten Boom Quotes," AZ Quotes, accessed June 29, 2015, http://www.azquotes.com/ quote/519578.
2. E. M. Bounds, *Power Through Prayer* (New York: Cosimo, 2007), 63.
3. Joel Osteen Ministries, accessed June 29, 2015, http://www.joelosteen.com/ downloadables/pages/downloads/thisismybible_jom.pdf.
4. Charles Spurgeon, "Infallibility—Where to Find It and How to Use It," sermon, December 20, 1874.
5. Brother Lawrence, *The Practice of the Presence of God: The Best Rule of Holy Life*, trans. Edgar G. Barton (London: Epworth), in "Fifth Letter," http://www.ccel.org/ccel/lawrence/ practice.iv.v.html.
6. Evelyn Underhill, *Practical Mysticism* (New York: E. P. Dutton & Company, 1915), in chapter 2, "The World of Reality," http://www.ccel.org/ccel/underhill/practical.vi.html.
7. Ibid.

Chapter 20: In the Wilderness

1. Joyce Meyer, "You Are What You Speak," ChristianPost.com, October 6, 2012, http://www .christianpost.com/news/you-are-what-you-speak-82817/.
2. C. S. Lewis, *The Screwtape Letters* in *The Complete C. S. Lewis Signature Classics* (New York: HarperOne, 2002), 208.
3. Charles Spurgeon, "The Underlying Gospel for the Dying Year," sermon, October 20, 1889.

Chapter 21: Eternity

1. Lewis, *Mere Christianity*, 112.
2. Thomas Moore, "Come, Ye Disconsolate," 1816, public domain.
3. Max Lucado, *When God Whispers Your Name* (Nashville: Thomas Nelson, 1999), 173

DARLENE ZSCHECH is acclaimed worldwide as a singer, songwriter, worship leader, and speaker. Although she has achieved numerous gold albums and her songs are sung in many nations, her success stands as a testimony to her life's passion to serve God and people with all her heart.

Mark and Darlene's life commitment to do whatever they can to bring answers and relief to human suffering prompted the birth of HOPE: Rwanda to bring hope and healing to that nation seemingly forgotten since the genocide of 1994. As this HOPE has spread into Cambodia, Vanuatu, India, Uganda, and beyond, their work through HOPE: Global continues to gather momentum.

In 2011, Mark and Darlene became senior pastors of Hope Unlimited Church on the beautiful Central Coast of New South Wales, where they now live with their family. While they travel extensively and have the honor of ministering around the globe, Darlene says, "First and foremost I am a woman who simply and wholeheartedly loves Christ, and serves Him through loving my family, serving the church in as many ways as I can, and speaking up for those who cannot speak for themselves."

FOR MORE INFORMATION, VISIT:
DARLENEZSCHECH.COM
HOPEUNLIMITEDCHURCH.COM.